MW01008788

Contents

Introduction

Whether you are new to the Blackstone griddle or are already a seasoned griddle pro, chances are you've seen the influence this popular cooking appliance has had on cooks everywhere—and the griddle craze continues to grow! Cooking on a griddle gives you a large, flat cooking space so you can prepare large quantities of food at once, and it makes feeding a crowd a breeze. But the best part is a griddle can cook almost anything—from seared meat and vegetables to fried rice, pizza, pasta, dips, and even desserts!

You can cook a meal more quickly on a Blackstone compared to indoors, because you can cook multiple dishes on different parts of the griddle at the same time. Also, because you use only one appliance instead of switching among multiple pans, cleanup is a cinch. Another bonus: During the hot months your kitchen can stay cool as you cook outside on your griddle. Blackstone cooking is also a healthier way to cook, because any grease produced drips off into the grease tray and stays away from your food.

At home, the Blackstone griddle helps with your backyard cooking and party needs and can be used for quick weekly meal prep. Away from home, Blackstone griddles are well known for the ease and variety they can bring to tailgate and camp cooking. Cooking over an open fire is unpredictable and sometimes dangerous, but an easily transported, safe griddle gives you many more options to enjoy tasty meals while experiencing the beauty of the outdoors. Whether you are at home or on the road, The "I Love My Blackstone Griddle" Cookbook will give you the information and ideas you need to make your griddle cooking a success!

The 175 recipes in this book provide a wide range of dishes, from super simple to more extravagant, to fit your needs for everything from easy weeknight meals to dishes guaranteed to wow your guests. You'll find energizing breakfasts, snacks to tide you over between meals, sides to pair with any entrée, satisfying main courses, meatless meals, and impressive desserts your guests will think you spent hours preparing. You'll also find appetizing photos, along with tips on seasoning your Blackstone and finding the right accessories to use with your griddle. And many recipes offer optional variations to make your griddle cooking an even more convenient and customizable experience. With so many delicious recipes to try, it's time to fire up your griddle and get things sizzling!

Cooking with a Blackstone Griddle

In this chapter you will learn all about your flat top griddle. Here, you'll find all the important information you need: instructions on seasoning your griddle, descriptions of must-have tools and accessories, helpful tips and tricks, and proper cleaning techniques.

What Is a Blackstone Griddle?

A Blackstone griddle is a flat steel cooking surface made to be used outdoors. Think of it as an extra-large cast iron skillet. Most flat top griddles run on propane, but some newer models are electric. The cooking surfaces come in various sizes, ranging from 17 inches all the way up to 36 inches. (If you have a smaller griddle, you may have to cook some of these recipes in batches, but the results will still be amazing.) Blackstone is just one of many brands of flat top griddles. You can use the recipes in this book for any brand of griddle you have.

A Blackstone griddle's large cooking space and heat zones allow you to cook large quantities of food *and* a wide range of different foods all at once, saving you both time and a sink full of dishes. A griddle is perfect for cooking for a crowd, meal prepping, camping or tailgate cooking, or just cooking in your own backyard.

There are a few things you need to do before you begin using your Blackstone griddle, and the most important (after setting it up) is seasoning your griddle.

Seasoning Your Griddle

Seasoning is the key to a long-lasting griddle. It creates a black coating on the surface that keeps food from sticking, prevents scratching and rust, and adds flavor to every meal you make. Griddle seasoning is very simple and is accomplished in three easy steps. You will need some dish soap, good quality paper towels, cooking oil, and tongs. A full tank of propane is recommended, because the process takes over an hour. You can use any cooking oil: olive oil, vegetable oil, avocado oil, or Blackstone's griddle seasoning and conditioning oil.

STEP 1 Wash the Surface

First, fill a small bowl with a drop of dish soap and some water. Dip a few paper towels into the soapy water, and use them to clean the griddle's surface thoroughly. This will remove any dust or dirt from shipping. To rinse, pour some clean water onto the griddle, wipe it clean with paper towels to remove any soapy residue, repeat a few times, and then dry completely.

STEP 2 Blacken the Griddle

Turn all burners on high heat for 15 minutes. You will notice some spots on the flat top start to darken slightly. Add 2–3 tablespoons of oil, depending on the size of your griddle. Use tongs to hold a paper towel or two, and spread the oil over the entire surface. Be sure to get the corners, edges, and outer edges of the griddle. The tongs will protect your hands; heat-resistant gloves are an added option. A very thin, smooth, and even layer of oil is key to keep food from sticking and prevent chipping.

Then sit back and relax as the griddle starts to blacken, which should take 10–15 minutes. This blackening process will create a good amount of smoke; this is normal and what you want to see.

Once the smoke stops, reapply another very thin, smooth layer of oil, spreading it with the paper towel and tongs just like in the first step. Wait another 10–15 minutes. Then apply one last coat of oil, waiting 10–15 minutes before turning your Blackstone off.

STEP 3 **Apply a Final Coat of Oil**

It is normal for the center of your griddle to be black, with the edges and corners a slightly lighter color. Not as much heat hits those areas, but after your first few cooks the entire surface will become the same blackened color.

After your griddle cools slightly, apply just one more very thin layer of oil, and use the tongs and paper towels to spread the oil evenly. Cover your griddle and it will be ready to go for your first cook!

Tools for Your Griddle

You're almost ready to start cooking on your new griddle, but first let's look at some tools and accessories. A few items are essential, and some will simply make your Blackstone griddle adventures easier and more comfortable. Here are the top tools and accessories to consider and the best uses for each.

Spatulas

Probably your most used tool will be a set of two hibachi spatulas—long, narrow spatulas made of thin metal, with handles. They are most used for stir-fries, fried rice, and flipping, and they can also be used for transferring food from the griddle. You can use both spatulas together to scoop stir-fries or use only one spatula for burgers. A friendly word of caution, though: It takes some practice to get the hang of using them. Just have fun with them, and after a few cooking sessions you'll be a pro.

Tongs

Tongs are used for placing or flipping food that's delicate or that doesn't have a flat surface—for example, kebabs, salmon, crostini, or some vegetables. You should invest in a longer pair of tongs, about 12–18 inches, to protect your hands from the flat top's heat while cooking and especially while seasoning your Blackstone.

Scraper

A griddle scraper is a thin, short piece of metal with a handle. Pretty much every time you use your griddle, you'll use this tool to push food particles to the grease cup to keep the griddle clean. Always remember to use the scraper gently to prevent any scratching of your griddle surface. You can also use the scraper to break up food, such as ground beef or chicken. Hold the scraper firmly and press down on the meat to chop or separate it as it cooks on the Blackstone.

Squeeze Bottles

It's handy to have at least two squeeze bottles at your outdoor cooking station: one with water and one with cooking oil. You will use both during every cook, so it's nice to have them handy and ready to go. Choose good-quality plastic bottles. Lids on the caps are a bonus. Keep them away from the griddle flame so the plastic doesn't melt.

Melting Dome

Some griddles come with a lid that lowers to keep the heat in. If your griddle doesn't have one, you'll need a melting dome. That's a metal dome a little over a foot wide, with a handle for easy lifting, used to melt cheese and to steam vegetables. Another option (and a good solution if what you want to cover is larger than your melting dome) is to use a disposable foil pan. Use caution with that, though; the pan may be extremely hot when it's time to remove it.

Burger Press

Another great tool for the Blackstone griddle is a small, round stainless steel burger press. Burger presses come in many varieties, but a stainless steel one is easier to clean and lighter in weight than a cast iron model. In addition to using your burger press to smash burgers, tacos, and potatoes, you can also use it to put pressure on or flatten bacon, wraps, and melted sandwiches.

Egg Rings

Egg rings are small, circular devices that keep food contained on the griddle. Metal egg rings are sometimes used, but silicone rings are easier to clean and do a better job of keeping food in place. Besides their classic use (cooking eggs for breakfast sandwiches) these neat tools can also be used to make cakes, brownies, and corn bread. I recommend buying a set of sixteen rings if you plan to do a lot of cakes and brownies.

Wind Guards

Depending on where you live and the time of year, you may want to invest in some wind guards for your griddle. These magnetic metal strips cover the area between the griddle and the stand. They block the wind to keep the flame going strong, and they keep the heat in during colder times of the year. This helps you use less propane while keeping the griddle temperature where you want it.

Storage Cart or Bin

You may want to get a cart or bin to store your outdoor cooking tools so they are easily accessible when cooking on your flat top. It will prevent many trips in and out of the house. In addition to holding your griddle tools and squirt bottles of water and oil, a cart is also a great place to keep a roll of paper towels, a pepper grinder, kosher salt, and a few other seasoning blends that you use often.

Protective Mat

It's inevitable that some grease spills and food splatters will happen when you're cooking on your griddle. A mat or floor protector under and around your cooking space will protect your deck or concrete. Any mat with a layer of rubber or plastic underneath will work just fine, but a heavier weight mat will stay put and won't blow in the wind.

Blackstone Griddle Cooking Tips and Tricks

Here are a few helpful hints about griddle cooking:

- First, and most importantly, preparation is key to successful and stress-free griddle cooking. Have your ingredients chopped and measured and packages open, because Blackstone cooking can go very fast.
- Put all your ingredients on a tray to carry them all easily outside to your cooking area. Most times you can use the same tray to transfer the meal back inside again.
- Preheating your griddle for several minutes is important. It can take 3–4 minutes for the griddle to properly preheat.
- Know your griddle hot spots and cooler areas. Typically, the center is the hottest and the edges are more on the warm side. Use those areas to your advantage by moving food around if something is cooking too quickly or not quickly enough.
- Outside temperatures can play a role in griddle surface temperatures. Adjust cooking times as needed based on the air temperature.
- You can cook an entire meal with multiple components on your Blackstone, but when you're first getting

started, keep things very simple. Begin with the easiest recipes and work your way up to becoming a griddle master!

Cleaning Your Blackstone Griddle

One of the best parts of griddle cooking is just how easy the cleanup is. It only takes three easy steps! Once you remove your food from your griddle, leave it on medium heat. The heat will make the cleaning process much easier and will prevent food particles from cooling and sticking. Most of the time you can clean your griddle right away—it takes less than a minute. But you can certainly enjoy the delicious meal that you prepared first and save cleanup for later.

STEP 1 Clear the Surface

First, use a scraper to remove any food that is still on the surface. The level of scraping will be determined by what you cooked or by how much mess is left. If there are just a few crumbs, you'll just need to use a dry paper towel or griddle scraper to push them into the grease cup. If you have a small amount of food stuck to your griddle, you may need to scrape a little more. Gentle scraping is always key to protect the surface.

For very messy situations, pour some water on your griddle and use the scraper to push everything into the grease cup. The water will help loosen any food or grease that has stuck. This is especially helpful when you've cooked with sticky or sweet sauces that may have burned on the surface.

STEP 2 Wipe the Surface Clean

Use a paper towel to dry and clean the surface. Be sure to get those corners and edges too. Use a good-quality brand of paper towels, or even heavy duty blue shop towels, to prevent any lint from sticking to your griddle. Since the surface is still hot, use tongs, not your hands, to hold the paper towel—or use your griddle scraper to push the paper towel around.

STEP 3 Oil the Surface

The final step is applying a thin coat of oil. Drizzle some oil, and use a dry paper towel to evenly spread it over the entire surface. You can use tongs or a griddle scraper to hold the paper towel as described in step 2. The thin oil layer will help protect the griddle surface from rust and ensure it stays well seasoned. A well-oiled griddle will also prevent food from sticking in the future.

Now that your griddle is clean and beautiful again, cover it back up and it will be all ready to go for your next griddle cook!

Breakfast

Mornings can be hectic, but fortunately with your Blackstone griddle you can whip up delicious and hearty breakfasts—sometimes even before your coffee is ready! This chapter offers a wide variety of delicious and easy-to-make breakfast, brunch, or even breakfast-for-dinner recipes for your griddle, including Chicken and Waffle Nachos, Pastrami Hash, Smashed Breakfast Tacos, Fluffy Buttermilk Pancakes, and Ham and Egg Breakfast Pizza. No matter what time of day, you will find lots of tasty options that are easy and quick to cook up on your Blackstone!

Sausage-Stuffed French Toast

This is not your traditional French toast recipe! This recipe calls for regular sausage links, but maple-flavored links would be a nice way to add even more flavor. You can also top this with scrambled eggs and cheese for a loaded version.

PREP TIME: 5 minutes   **COOK TIME: 14 minutes**   **SERVES: 6**

12 breakfast sausage links

6 hot dog buns

2 large eggs

1/4 cup 2% milk

1 tablespoon granulated sugar

1 teaspoon vanilla extract

2 tablespoons unsalted butter

1/2 tablespoon confectioners' sugar

1/2 cup pure maple syrup

Adding More Flavor

There is such a wide variety of flavored coffee creamers available on the market today. Use your favorite in the French toast batter in place of the milk. You can create many different flavor options with this simple substitution.

1. Preheat griddle to medium-low. Add sausage links to griddle and cook 7–8 minutes, turning a few times with tongs, until cooked through. Remove links from griddle and put 2 links in each bun. Press down with your hands or a spatula to slightly flatten buns.

2. In a medium bowl, whisk eggs, milk, granulated sugar, and vanilla until combined.

3. Add butter to Blackstone and allow it to melt. Dip each sausage-stuffed bun into egg mixture for a few seconds and then place it on griddle.

4. Cook each bun for 2–3 minutes per side until golden brown, pressing with a spatula to flatten slightly.

5. Remove from griddle, sprinkle confectioners' sugar on top, and serve with maple syrup for dipping.

PER SERVING
Calories: **435**
Fat: **9g**
Protein: **13g**
Sodium: **657mg**
Fiber: **1g**
Carbohydrates: **42g**
Sugar: **22g**

Pastrami Hash

Move over, corned beef! Pastrami hash is the new, delicious take on a classic breakfast dish. This hearty hash is also perfect topped with fried eggs as a bonus. Make your eggs right on the griddle and serve them on top of the hash.

PREP TIME: 10 minutes   **COOK TIME: 12 minutes**   **SERVES: 6**

2 tablespoons vegetable oil

1 (28-ounce) bag frozen diced potatoes, thawed

1 medium yellow onion, peeled and diced

1 medium red bell pepper, seeded and diced

2 medium jalapeño peppers, seeded and diced

1/2 teaspoon kosher salt

1/4 teaspoon ground black pepper

1/2 teaspoon Cajun seasoning

1 pound deli pastrami, diced

4 cloves garlic, peeled and minced

1. Preheat griddle to medium. Add oil, then potatoes, onion, bell and jalapeño peppers, salt, black pepper, and Cajun seasoning. Cook 8 minutes, mixing with spatulas.

2. Add pastrami and garlic. Cook and mix 3–4 more minutes until hash is as crisp as you like. Serve warm.

PER SERVING
Calories: **264**
Fat: **8g**
Protein: **20g**
Sodium: **791mg**
Fiber: **3g**
Carbohydrates: **30g**
Sugar: **2g**

Green Chile Breakfast Tacos

These tacos are a fun breakfast or brunch that's great for feeding a crowd. You can even set up a topping bar with sour cream, cheese, cilantro, and salsa so everyone can make their own unique tacos. You can also substitute flour tortillas for corn if you like.

PREP TIME: 10 minutes   **COOK TIME: 11 minutes**   **SERVES: 8**

8 large eggs

1/2 teaspoon kosher salt

1/4 teaspoon ground black pepper

2 tablespoons vegetable oil, divided

1 pound ground breakfast sausage

1 medium red bell pepper, seeded and diced

1 medium yellow onion, peeled and diced

1 (4-ounce) can diced green chiles

16 (5-inch) corn tortillas

Idea for Leftovers

This recipe makes a lot, so if you're not feeding a crowd, you can make breakfast burritos with any leftovers. Simply roll extra filling into a flour tortilla, wrap in plastic wrap or foil, and store in the refrigerator or freezer. Reheat in the microwave for an easy breakfast.

1. Crack eggs into a medium bowl, add salt and pepper, and beat with a fork.
2. Preheat griddle to medium. Add 1 tablespoon oil, sausage, peppers, and onions. Cook 7 minutes, breaking up meat and mixing ingredients with spatulas.
3. Add green chiles and slowly pour eggs over sausage mixture. Cook and scramble until eggs are set, about 2 minutes.
4. Remove from griddle and set aside. Scrape griddle clean. Add remaining 1 tablespoon oil and arrange tortillas on griddle to warm, cooking 1–2 minutes and flipping each a few times.
5. Fill tortillas with egg mixture and serve.

PER SERVING

Calories: **372**

Fat: **23g**

Protein: **15g**

Sodium: **754mg**

Fiber: **4g**

Carbohydrates: **25g**

Sugar: **2g**

Fluffy Buttermilk Pancakes

This homemade pancake recipe creates a light and airy pancake with crispy edges. For a complete breakfast try making some bacon or sausage on the griddle too.

PREP TIME: 10 minutes   **COOK TIME: 5 minutes**   **SERVES: 4**

2 cups all-purpose flour

2 cups 1% buttermilk

2 large eggs, beaten

3 tablespoons granulated sugar

2 teaspoons baking soda

1/8 teaspoon kosher salt

2 tablespoons unsalted butter

1/3 cup pure maple syrup

1. To a medium bowl, add flour, buttermilk, eggs, sugar, baking soda, and salt. Stir until just combined—do not overmix.

2. Preheat griddle to medium-low. Add butter and, once melted, spoon batter onto griddle to make 8 equal pancakes. Cook 2–3 minutes per side until golden brown. Serve right away with maple syrup.

Pancake Additions

Ideas for pancake additions are endless. Try fresh blueberries or sliced bananas, or make it even sweeter with chocolate chips, fruity cereal, or crushed chocolate sandwich cookies. Anything you choose to add, just sprinkle it over the batter right after it hits the griddle. You could even make s'mores pancakes by including crushed graham crackers, mini marshmallows, and chocolate chips.

PER SERVING

Calories: **454**

Fat: **8g**

Protein: **14g**

Sodium: **962mg**

Fiber: **2g**

Carbohydrates: **81g**

Sugar: **31g**

Jammy Monte Cristo Melts

This fruity twist on the classic sandwich makes a nice brunch or breakfast-for-dinner. For added crunch and a pop of texture, you can also coat these in a crushed-up breakfast cereal of your choice right after dipping them in the eggs.

PREP TIME: 15 minutes   **COOK TIME: 5 minutes**   **SERVES: 4**

2 ounces blackberry jam

8 (1-ounce) slices brioche

8 (1-ounce) slices Swiss cheese

12 (1-ounce) slices deli ham

2 large eggs

$1/4$ cup 2% milk

1 tablespoon granulated sugar

1 teaspoon vanilla extract

2 tablespoons unsalted butter

$1/2$ tablespoon confectioners' sugar

1. To assemble each sandwich, spread $1/4$ of the jam on a slice of bread, then add a slice of cheese, 3 slices of ham, another slice of cheese, and a top slice of bread. Repeat with remaining ingredients.
2. Crack eggs into a medium bowl. Add milk, sugar, and vanilla and whisk until combined.
3. Preheat griddle to medium-low. Add butter to griddle and allow to melt. Dip each sandwich into egg mixture for a few seconds on both sides. Place on griddle and cook 2–3 minutes per side until golden brown.
4. Sprinkle confectioners' sugar on top and serve.

PER SERVING

Calories: **609**

Fat: **26g**

Protein: **37g**

Sodium: **1,153mg**

Fiber: **0g**

Carbohydrates: **51g**

Sugar: **18g**

Ham, Egg, and Cheese Breakfast Bombs

This recipe idea promises an explosion of flavor: individually wrapped biscuit packages filled with all your breakfast favorites. You can easily substitute cooked sausage or bacon in place of the ham if desired.

PREP TIME: **15 minutes**   COOK TIME: **25 minutes**   SERVES: **4**

3 large eggs

3 tablespoons 2% milk

$1/4$ teaspoon kosher salt

$1/8$ teaspoon ground black pepper

1 cup diced deli ham

3 tablespoons unsalted butter, divided

1 cup shredded Cheddar cheese

1 (16-ounce, 8-count) tube refrigerated jumbo biscuits

1 tablespoon pure maple syrup

1. Crack eggs into a small bowl. Add milk, salt, and pepper, and whisk until combined.
2. Preheat griddle to medium-low. Add ham and allow to cook 2 minutes. Add 1 tablespoon butter and, once melted, slowly pour eggs over ham. Scramble mixture on griddle with spatulas for about 2 minutes until eggs are set. Mix in cheese and cook 1 more minute. Turn Blackstone off and remove egg mixture. Turning the griddle off allows it time to cool for the next step.
3. Roll biscuits as flat as you can get them. Add $1/8$ of filling in the center of each biscuit, and then stretch and fold dough around filling, overlapping edges slightly to seal. Roll each into a ball.
4. Preheat griddle to lowest heat setting. Place biscuit balls on griddle surface, seam sides down, and cover with melting dome or lid for 9 minutes. Flip and cover again for 9–10 more minutes until dough is golden brown and cooked through.
5. Melt remaining 2 tablespoons butter on griddle and mix with maple syrup. Brush mixture over biscuits and serve.

PER SERVING

Calories: **635**

Fat: **26g**

Protein: **25g**

Sodium: **2,017mg**

Fiber: **2g**

Carbohydrates: **53g**

Sugar: **8g**

Bacon Pancake Dippers

This fun breakfast requires no utensils. The recipe uses a store-bought box of pancake mix to keep it very simple, but you could certainly use homemade pancake batter if you prefer.

PREP TIME: 5 minutes   **COOK TIME: 12 minutes**   **SERVES: 4**

8 slices bacon

2 cups prepared pancake batter

$1/4$ cup pure maple syrup

Helpful Tips

Use a $1/4$-cup measuring cup with a handle to pour the pancake batter. That will ensure each slice of bacon has the same amount of batter and make it easier to pour each portion in one shot. Once the pancake batter begins to bubble, then you know it's the perfect time to flip.

1. Preheat griddle to medium-low. Place bacon on griddle. Cook 5–7 minutes, flipping a few times until cooked to your taste. Move bacon to one side of griddle, and gently scrape some of the bacon grease into the grease cup.
2. Move bacon back to center of griddle, leaving some space between slices. Pour $1/8$ of the pancake batter over each bacon slice, covering each completely.
3. Cook 2–3 minutes per side until pancake batter is cooked through and as brown as you like. Serve with maple syrup for dipping.

PER SERVING

Calories: **338**
Fat: **10g**
Protein: **12g**

Sodium: **877mg**
Fiber: **1g**
Carbohydrates: **48g**
Sugar: **19g**

Sausage and Egg Breakfast Sliders

If you like cheeseburger sliders, then you'll love these breakfast sliders. You can add slices of cooked bacon for even more meat. Try drizzling maple syrup and a few dashes of hot sauce on top of the cheese in step 5 for a sweet and spicy sauce.

PREP TIME: 10 minutes   **COOK TIME: 12 minutes**   **SERVES: 4**

6 large eggs

1/4 teaspoon kosher salt

1/8 teaspoon ground black pepper

1 pound ground breakfast sausage

1 tablespoon unsalted butter

1 (12-count) package sweet slider buns, not separated, sliced horizontally to separate tops from bottoms

1 1/2 cups shredded Cheddar cheese

1. Crack eggs into a medium bowl, add salt and pepper, and beat with a fork.
2. Shape sausage into one large, rectangular patty slightly larger than the slider buns.
3. Preheat griddle to medium-low. Melt butter and slowly pour on eggs. Scramble eggs with spatulas about 2 minutes, then remove and set aside.
4. Place sausage patty on griddle. Cook 3–4 minutes per side until cooked through.
5. Turn griddle off. Add both bun halves, cut sides down, to griddle for a few seconds. Flip bottom bun half over and add sausage, eggs, and cheese.
6. Cover with a melting dome or lid 1–2 minutes until cheese is melted. Remove dome and add top bun half. Cut into individual buns before serving.

PER SERVING
Calories: **886**
Fat: **57g**
Protein: **40g**
Sodium: **1,786mg**
Fiber: **1g**
Carbohydrates: **47g**
Sugar: **15g**

Ham and Egg Breakfast Pizza

The best part of this pizza is when you cut into the egg and discover the saucy, rich, and luscious yolk. Yum! Feel free to use bacon or sausage in place of the ham if you prefer.

PREP TIME: **10 minutes**   COOK TIME: **12 minutes**   SERVES: **4**

1 pound pizza dough

1 tablespoon olive oil

2 tablespoons pure maple syrup

2 cups shredded Cheddar cheese

$1/2$ pound diced ham

1 tablespoon unsalted butter

4 large eggs

$1/4$ teaspoon kosher salt

$1/8$ teaspoon ground black pepper

Griddle Pizza Dough

Cook time for pizza dough on the griddle largely depends on the thickness of your crust. Try to occasionally peek at the bottom of the crust during cooking to make sure it's not browning too quickly. If so, simply turn heat to low, or even turn the griddle off to allow time for the cheese to melt under the melting dome.

1. Roll pizza dough into a circle approximately 16 inches across.
2. Preheat griddle to medium-low. Add oil and then pizza dough. Allow dough to cook about 2 minutes, depending on crust thickness, and then flip.
3. Drizzle on maple syrup, then sprinkle cheese and ham on top. Cover with a melting dome or lid for 5–8 minutes. Remove once cheese is melted and crust is cooked through.
4. Add butter to an empty space on griddle. Once melted, crack eggs onto griddle, season them with salt and pepper, and cook about 1 minute per side or until cooked to your liking. Add fried eggs to top of pizza.
5. Remove pizza from griddle, slice, and serve.

PER SERVING

Calories: **746**

Fat: **34g**

Protein: **41g**

Sodium: **2,004mg**

Fiber: **2g**

Carbohydrates: **62g**

Sugar: **13g**

Cheesy Chorizo Pancakes

You can use either a pancake mix or homemade batter for these sweet and spicy pancakes. Not a fan of chorizo? Use breakfast sausage instead.

PREP TIME: 10 minutes   **COOK TIME: 11 minutes**   **SERVES: 4**

1/2 pound ground chorizo

2 cups prepared pancake batter

1 cup shredded Cheddar cheese

2 tablespoons unsalted butter

1/4 cup pure maple syrup

1/2 tablespoon hot sauce

PER SERVING
Calories: **625**
Fat: **31g**
Protein: **22g**
Sodium: **1,590mg**
Fiber: **1g**
Carbohydrates: **60g**
Sugar: **21g**

1. Preheat griddle to medium. Add chorizo to griddle and cook 5 minutes, breaking apart with spatulas. Remove, scrape griddle, and set heat to medium-low.
2. In a large bowl, mix cooked chorizo, pancake batter, and cheese until combined.
3. Add butter to griddle. Spoon batter mixture onto Blackstone to make 8 pancakes. Cook 2–3 minutes per side until golden brown.
4. Mix maple syrup and hot sauce together in a small bowl and serve with pancakes.

Simple Sausage Biscuits

These mini breakfast sandwiches are easy to make all at once on the griddle. You can reheat them for breakfast on the go. Add cheese and egg to jazz them up.

PREP TIME: 10 minutes   **COOK TIME: 9 minutes**   **SERVES: 5**

1 pound ground breakfast sausage

1 (7.5-ounce, 10-count) tube refrigerated biscuits

PER SERVING
Calories: **392**
Fat: **29g**
Protein: **12g**
Sodium: **1,215mg**
Fiber: **1g**
Carbohydrates: **21g**
Sugar: **3g**

1. Divide and shape sausage into 10 patties. Open tube and separate biscuits.
2. Preheat griddle to medium-low. Place biscuits to one side and patties on the other.
3. Cook 7–9 minutes, flipping several times with spatulas. Once biscuits are golden brown, move them to the edge to stay warm while sausage finishes cooking through.
4. Slice each biscuit in half, place a sausage patty between the halves to make a sausage biscuit sandwich and serve.

Strawberries and Cream French Toast

What's better than regular French toast? French toast filled with berries and cream, of course. You can also mix this recipe up with blueberries, bananas, or another fruit.

PREP TIME: **15 minutes**   COOK TIME: **6 minutes**   SERVES: **4**

6 ounces whipped cream cheese, at room temperature

8 (1-ounce) slices brioche

1 cup sliced strawberries

2 large eggs

1/4 cup 2% milk

1 tablespoon granulated sugar

1 teaspoon vanilla extract

2 tablespoons unsalted butter

1 tablespoon confectioners' sugar

1. Spread cream cheese on 4 slices of bread. Lay strawberries on top of cream cheese, then add top piece of bread to each sandwich, pressing down slightly.
2. Crack eggs into a medium bowl. Add milk, granulated sugar, and vanilla and whisk until combined.
3. Preheat griddle to medium-low. Add butter and, once melted, dip each sandwich into egg mixture, coating both sides, then place each on griddle. Cook 2–3 minutes per side until golden brown.
4. Sprinkle confectioners' sugar on top and serve.

PER SERVING
Calories: **378**
Fat: **17g**
Protein: **10g**
Sodium: **491mg**
Fiber: **1g**
Carbohydrates: **45g**
Sugar: **14g**

Chorizo Potatoes and Eggs

This recipe is a simple, spicy breakfast to make on the Blackstone. For a milder version you could substitute ground breakfast sausage, poblano peppers, and Cheddar cheese.

PREP TIME: 10 minutes   **COOK TIME: 16 minutes**   **SERVES: 6**

1 tablespoon vegetable oil

1 (28-ounce) bag frozen diced potatoes, thawed

1/2 teaspoon kosher salt

1 pound ground chorizo

3 medium jalapeño peppers, seeded and diced

2 cups shredded pepper jack cheese

1 tablespoon unsalted butter

6 large eggs

1. Preheat griddle to medium. Add oil, potatoes, and salt. Cook 3 minutes, mixing with spatulas.
2. Add chorizo and jalapeños. Cook 9 more minutes, using spatulas to break chorizo apart. Add cheese, mix, and cook 1 more minute until cheese is melted. Remove from griddle, set aside, and scrape griddle clean.
3. Add butter to griddle and, once melted, crack eggs onto griddle. Cook 2–3 minutes, flipping halfway through cooking time, and remove once cooked to your taste. Serve fried eggs over the chorizo and potatoes.

PER SERVING
Calories: **679**
Fat: **46g**
Protein: **37g**
Sodium: **1,429mg**
Fiber: **2g**
Carbohydrates: **23g**
Sugar: **1g**

Chicken and Waffle Nachos

Chicken and waffles, flat top griddle–style! This recipe is an easy way to enjoy this traditional breakfast or brunch with a unique flair. Top with hot sauce and sliced jalapeños if you'd like a sweet and spicy version. Forks may be required.

PREP TIME: **10 minutes**   COOK TIME: **9 minutes**   SERVES: **4**

2 large eggs

1 tablespoon 2% milk

1/4 teaspoon kosher salt

1/8 teaspoon ground black pepper

1 tablespoon unsalted butter

4 frozen toaster waffles, thawed

2 frozen chicken patties, thawed

1/2 cup shredded Cheddar cheese

1/4 cup pure maple syrup

1. Crack eggs into a medium bowl and add milk, salt, and pepper. Whisk until combined.
2. Preheat griddle to medium-low. Melt butter and slowly pour on egg mixture. Use spatulas to scramble eggs until set, about 2 minutes. Remove and set aside.
3. Put waffles and chicken patties on griddle. Cook waffles 3–4 minutes, flipping a few times; remove when they are crisp. Cook chicken 6 minutes, flipping a few times, until crisp. Remove chicken.
4. Cut waffles into fourths and dice chicken. Put waffles back onto griddle and top each with eggs, chicken, and cheese. Cover with melting dome or lid about 1 minute until cheese is melted.
5. Drizzle with maple syrup and serve right away.

PER SERVING

Calories: **362**

Fat: **18g**

Protein: **14g**

Sodium: **645mg**

Fiber: **0g**

Carbohydrates: **33g**

Sugar: **13g**

Cinnamon Sugar Donuts

People often deep-fry or air fry biscuit dough to make donuts, but you can also make them on the Blackstone. They come out amazingly delicious, and they're very easy to make in just a few minutes.

PREP TIME: 15 minutes   **COOK TIME: 11 minutes**   **SERVES: 4**

1 (16-ounce, 8-count) tube refrigerated jumbo biscuits

1/2 cup granulated sugar

1 tablespoon ground cinnamon

4 tablespoons unsalted butter, divided

Donut Toppings

In place of the cinnamon sugar, you have some additional options for topping the donuts. You could mix confectioners' sugar with a very small amount of milk to make a glaze. To take it further, top the glazed donuts with chopped pecans or bacon bits! Another possibility: Spread cake icing on the donuts and add sprinkles.

1. Use a 1-inch cutter or bottle lid to make a hole in the center of each biscuit. Place sugar and cinnamon in a medium bowl and stir until combined.

2. Preheat griddle to medium-low. Add 1 tablespoon butter and, once melted, place biscuit rings and holes on griddle. Cover with a melting dome or lid for 5 minutes. Flip and cover again for 5–6 more minutes until golden brown and cooked through.

3. Put remaining 3 tablespoons butter in a small bowl, microwave 30 seconds or until melted, and brush on all sides of donuts and donut holes. Use a spoon to toss donuts and holes, a few at a time, in cinnamon sugar. Best if served right away.

PER SERVING
Calories: **484**
Fat: **13g**
Protein: **7g**

Sodium: **1,209mg**
Fiber: **2g**
Carbohydrates: **68g**
Sugar: **24g**

Steak and Egg Breakfast Quesadillas

Steak and eggs is a classic breakfast combination for when you really need a hearty meal to start your day. These quesadillas use those well-loved flavors, and they can be made in advance and reheated throughout the week. They're great topped with sour cream.

PREP TIME: 10 minutes **COOK TIME: 12 minutes** **SERVES: 4**

6 large eggs

$1/4$ cup 2% milk

$1/2$ teaspoon kosher salt, divided

$1/4$ teaspoon ground black pepper, divided

2 tablespoons vegetable oil, divided

1 pound sirloin steak, cut into bite-sized pieces

4 (10-inch) flour tortillas

3 cups shredded Cheddar cheese

1. Crack eggs into a medium bowl, add milk , $1/4$ teaspoon salt, and $1/8$ teaspoon pepper, and whisk until combined.
2. Preheat griddle to medium-low. Add $1/2$ tablespoon oil and slowly pour on eggs. Use spatulas to scramble eggs until set, about 2 minutes. Remove from griddle and set aside.
3. Add $1/2$ tablespoon oil, steak, remaining $1/4$ teaspoon salt, and $1/8$ teaspoon pepper to griddle. Cook 4 minutes or until steak is cooked how you prefer, mixing a few times. Remove from griddle.
4. Add remaining 1 tablespoon oil to griddle and lay each tortilla flat on griddle. Evenly distribute half of the cheese among the tortillas, covering half of each tortilla, then do the same with all of the eggs, the steak, and the remaining cheese. Use spatulas to fold each tortilla's empty half over the fillings, creating a half-moon shape.
5. Cook 2–3 minutes per side or until cheese is melted and tortilla is as crisp as you like. Slice and serve.

PER SERVING

Calories: **947**

Fat: **52g**

Protein: **62g**

Sodium: **1,463mg**

Fiber: **2g**

Carbohydrates: **39g**

Sugar: **3g**

Smashed Breakfast Tacos

If you've never met a taco you didn't like, why not enjoy them for your next weekend breakfast or brunch? Eggs, cheese, and sausage in a cheesy tortilla—it doesn't get yummier than this. Try topping them with sour cream for a savory version, or with a drizzle of maple syrup to sweeten things up a bit.

PREP TIME: 10 minutes   **COOK TIME: 8 minutes**   **SERVES: 4**

3 large eggs

2 tablespoons 2% milk

1/4 teaspoon kosher salt

1/8 teaspoon ground black pepper

1 pound ground breakfast sausage

1 tablespoon unsalted butter

8 (6-inch) flour tortillas

1 cup shredded Cheddar cheese

1. Crack eggs into a small bowl, add milk, salt, and pepper, and beat with a fork. Roll sausage into 8 balls.

2. Preheat griddle to medium-low. Add butter and, once melted, slowly pour on eggs. Scramble with spatulas and cook about 2 minutes until eggs are set. Remove from griddle, set aside, and scrape griddle if needed.

3. Raise heat to medium. Place sausage balls on Blackstone, spaced 6-inches apart. Lay a tortilla over each sausage ball, and use a burger press to smash the meat flat. Cook 4 minutes, then flip and cook 1–2 more minutes until tortilla is crisped to your liking.

4. Top with eggs and cheese, fold in half like a taco, and serve right away.

PER SERVING

Calories: **661**

Fat: **17g**

Protein: **33g**

Sodium: **1,522mg**

Fiber: **2g**

Carbohydrates: **33g**

Sugar: **3g**

Donut Bacon Melts

This dish is a great trio of sweet, salty, and cheesy! It is a perfect use for leftover glazed donuts. These melts are also messy, but in the most fun way. Add an egg for an even heartier meal.

PREP TIME: 5 minutes   **COOK TIME: 13 minutes**   **SERVES: 4**

8 slices bacon

2 tablespoons unsalted butter

4 glazed donuts, cut in half to separate tops and bottoms

8 (1-ounce) slices American cheese

Work Smarter, Not Harder

Many recipes in this book, such as this one, call for bacon. If you're planning a few meals or appetizers that require bacon, try prepping a big batch early in the week so you don't have to cook it for every recipe. Preheat your Blackstone to medium-low, add as many bacon slices as you'd like, and cook 5–7 minutes, flipping a few times. Once it's crisped to your liking, remove from the griddle, cool, crumble, and store in the refrigerator in a covered container until needed.

1. Preheat griddle to medium-low. Place bacon on griddle and cook 5–7 minutes, flipping a few times until it reaches your desired doneness. Remove from griddle and scrape most of the grease away.
2. Melt butter on griddle, then place bottom half of each donut on griddle, cut-side down. Add to each a slice of cheese, 2 slices bacon, and another slice of cheese. Top each with remaining half of donut, cut-side up.
3. Cook 2–3 minutes per side, pressing down a few times with spatulas to melt cheese. Remove once donuts are golden brown. Serve warm.

PER SERVING

Calories: **460**

Fat: **29g**

Protein: **19g**

Sodium: **1,300mg**

Fiber: **0g**

Carbohydrates: **27g**

Sugar: **13g**

Breakfast Fried Rice

It may seem unusual to have fried rice for breakfast, but it is delicious. This version has more eggs than a traditional fried rice, and it uses Japanese barbecue sauce, a sweet, soy-flavored sauce that's available in many stores and tastes nothing like traditional American barbecue sauce.

PREP TIME: 10 minutes　　**COOK TIME: 12 minutes**　　**SERVES: 8**

6 tablespoons unsalted butter, divided

1 medium yellow onion, peeled and diced

1 medium red bell pepper, seeded and diced

6 cups cooked, cooled jasmine rice

1 pound deli ham, diced

6 large eggs

4 tablespoons Japanese barbecue sauce

2 tablespoons soy sauce

4 medium scallions, sliced

1. Preheat griddle to medium. Melt 3 tablespoons butter. Add onion and pepper to griddle. Cook 3 minutes, mixing a few times with spatulas.
2. Add rice and ham and stir to combine. Crack eggs over mixture. Cook 3 minutes, mixing with spatulas and breaking eggs apart.
3. Add remaining 3 tablespoons butter, Japanese barbecue sauce, soy sauce, and scallions. Continue cooking and mixing 5–6 more minutes until rice is cooked to your liking. Serve immediately.

PER SERVING

Calories: **386**

Fat: **15g**

Protein: **19g**

Sodium: **1,262mg**

Fiber: **2g**

Carbohydrates: **39g**

Sugar: **5g**

Breakfast Pigs in a Blanket

Kids will love this sweet and savory breakfast. Use toothpicks to hold the "blankets" closed as they cook on the Blackstone (just remember to remove the toothpicks before serving).

PREP TIME: 10 minutes   **COOK TIME: 23 minutes**   **SERVES: 4**

8 breakfast sausage links

1 (12.4-ounce, 8-count) tube refrigerated cinnamon rolls, with icing

1. Preheat griddle to medium-low. Add sausage links and cook 7–8 minutes, turning a few times with tongs. Once cooked through, remove and set aside. Turn heat to lowest setting.
2. Roll each cinnamon bun as flat as possible. Place a sausage link in the center of each and roll it up, overlapping the dough, with the ends of the sausage sticking out. Insert a toothpick through the center to hold in place.
3. Place on Blackstone, cover with melting dome or lid, and cook 7 minutes. Flip, cover again, and cook for 7–8 more minutes until golden brown and cooked through.
4. Drizzle with icing before serving.

PER SERVING

Calories: **439**

Fat: **15g**

Protein: **12g**

Sodium: **1,060mg**

Fiber: **1g**

Carbohydrates: **48g**

Sugar: **19g**

CHAPTER 3

Appetizers and Snacks

In this chapter you will find tons of appetizers for tailgating, parties, or holidays, or just to enjoy as fun weekend snacks. You'll find a variety of options, such as Bacon Jalapeño Corn Dip, Chicken Wings, Cheesy Meatball Sliders, Bacon-Wrapped Barbecue Chicken Bites, Bang-Bang Shrimp, and Loaded Soft Pretzel Bites. You'll also discover presentation tips and many dishes that can easily be transported or prepared in advance. With so many delicious possibilities, you may have trouble deciding which of the snacks and appetizers to bring to your next social event!

Sausage-Stuffed Jalapeño Poppers

Cheesy stuffed jalapeños are the ultimate game-day appetizer. This recipe makes a lot, so it's perfect for parties. You can make them a day ahead and warm them back up on the griddle over medium heat for 5–6 minutes, covered with a melting dome or lid.

PREP TIME: 15 minutes **COOK TIME: 19 minutes** **SERVES: 10**

20 large jalapeño peppers

1 pound ground Italian sausage

1 medium yellow onion, peeled and diced

8 ounces cream cheese

1 cup shredded Cheddar cheese

1/2 teaspoon kosher salt

Preparing the Jalapeños

It is recommended that you wear gloves to cut and seed the jalapeños in case your skin is sensitive. Use a spoon to scrape out the seeds and white ribs, and to protect your eyes make sure to direct the scraping away from your face. If you like your poppers a little spicier, leave some seeds in the peppers.

1. Slice each jalapeño in half lengthwise and remove seeds and white ribs.
2. Preheat griddle to medium. Add peppers, cut sides down, and cook for 5 minutes. Remove and set aside.
3. Add sausage and onion to griddle. Cook, breaking sausage apart with spatulas, for 8 minutes. Turn Blackstone off and transfer mixture to a medium bowl.
4. Add cream cheese, Cheddar, and salt to bowl with sausage and mix until combined. Stuff mixture evenly into each jalapeño half.
5. Preheat griddle to medium. Place jalapeños back on griddle, stuffed sides up, for 5–6 more minutes, covering with a melting dome or lid, until jalapeños are soft and filling is warm. Serve warm or at room temperature.

PER SERVING

Calories: **260**

Fat: **19g**

Protein: **11g**

Sodium: **690mg**

Fiber: **1g**

Carbohydrates: **5g**

Sugar: **3g**

Chorizo Cheese Dip

This recipe makes a big batch of dip! You can easily halve it if needed. Serve this with plenty of tortilla chips or scoop-shaped corn chips for dipping. It can also be made in advance and warmed up.

PREP TIME: 10 minutes   **COOK TIME: 13 minutes**   **SERVES: 14**

2 pounds ground chorizo

1 medium yellow onion, peeled and diced

6 cloves garlic, peeled and minced

2 (8-ounce) blocks cream cheese

1 (15-ounce) jar salsa

1. Preheat griddle to medium. Add chorizo, onion, and garlic to griddle and cook 8 minutes, breaking chorizo apart with spatulas as it cooks.
2. Put cream cheese and salsa in a 9-inch-by-13-inch foil pan or a 12-inch cast iron skillet. Transfer chorizo to pan or skillet. Scrape griddle clean.
3. Place pan or skillet on Blackstone. Cook 4–5 minutes, stirring mixture until it's combined and melted together. Serve warm.

PER SERVING

Calories: **289**

Fat: **23g**

Protein: **15g**

Sodium: **977mg**

Fiber: **1g**

Carbohydrates: **4g**

Sugar: **3g**

Crispy Beef Mini Tacos

The key to this recipe is getting that crispy taco shell, so you may need to add more oil to achieve maximum crispiness. Serve these with salsa and/or guacamole for dipping. If you are making these in advance, warm them up on the griddle for a few minutes over medium heat.

PREP TIME: 5 minutes   **COOK TIME: 10 minutes**   **SERVES: 6**

1 pound 80/20 ground beef

3 tablespoons taco seasoning

2 tablespoons vegetable oil

18 (5-inch) corn tortillas

3 cups shredded Cheddar cheese

1. Preheat griddle to medium. Add beef and cook, breaking meat apart with spatulas, for 6 minutes or until cooked through. During the last 2 minutes of cooking time, add taco seasoning and $1/4$ cup water and mix it all together. Remove beef, scrape griddle, and lower heat to medium-low.

2. Add oil and tortillas to griddle. Place some beef and cheese on one half of each tortilla. Use spatulas to fold each tortilla in half, creating a half-moon shape. Cook 3–4 minutes, flipping a few times. Once crisped to your taste, remove and serve.

PER SERVING

Calories: **574**

Fat: **29g**

Protein: **32g**

Sodium: **752mg**

Fiber: **5g**

Carbohydrates: **35g**

Sugar: **1g**

Loaded Soft Pretzel Bites

You can easily find soft pretzel bites in the bakery section of most large grocery stores. This recipe gives those traditional bites a makeover on the Blackstone. For extra cheesiness, try dipping them in warm nacho cheese sauce.

PREP TIME: **5 minutes**   COOK TIME: **10 minutes**   SERVES: **6**

8 slices bacon

1 (12-ounce) package soft pretzel
  bites

2$\frac{1}{2}$ cups shredded Cheddar cheese

4 medium scallions, sliced

$\frac{1}{2}$ cup ranch dressing

1. Preheat griddle to medium-low. Place bacon on griddle and cook 5–7 minutes, flipping a few times, until bacon is as crisp as you like. Remove and let cool. Crumble and set aside.
2. Scrape away some of the bacon grease. Put pretzel bites on griddle and cook 3 minutes, flipping a few times with spatulas, until warmed through.
3. Arrange bites on griddle, touching but in a single layer. Top with cheese, scallions, and crumbled bacon. Cover with a melting dome or lid for 1 more minute until cheese is melted.
4. Drizzle with ranch dressing and serve right away.

PER SERVING

Calories: **417**
Fat: **19g**
Protein: **21g**

Sodium: **694mg**
Fiber: **1g**
Carbohydrates: **33g**
Sugar: **1g**

Tomato Burrata Crostini

Here is a fancy appetizer with a showstopping presentation. These can be prepared a few hours in advance and served at room temperature. For some color, try garnishing them with fresh basil or arugula. Fresh mozzarella could be used in place of the burrata.

PREP TIME: 10 minutes　　**COOK TIME: 9 minutes**　　**SERVES: 5**

3 tablespoons olive oil, divided

2 pints grape tomatoes (whole)

2 tablespoons balsamic vinegar

$1/2$ teaspoon kosher salt, divided

$1/4$ teaspoon ground black pepper, divided

1 (16-ounce) loaf French bread, sliced into 20 pieces

12 ounces burrata

2 ounces balsamic glaze

1. Preheat griddle to medium. Add 1 tablespoon oil, tomatoes, vinegar, $1/4$ teaspoon salt, and $1/8$ teaspoon pepper. Cook 7 minutes, mixing with spatulas.

2. Remove from griddle and set aside. Scrape griddle clean. Add remaining 2 tablespoons oil to griddle, then bread slices. Cook 45 seconds per side, or until toasted to your liking.

3. To assemble crostini, tear burrata and distribute evenly among bread slices, then top each with a few tomatoes. Drizzle with balsamic glaze and season with remaining $1/4$ teaspoon salt and $1/8$ teaspoon pepper. Serve.

PER SERVING

Calories: **566**

Fat: **24g**

Protein: **22g**

Sodium: **948mg**

Fiber: **3g**

Carbohydrates: **61g**

Sugar: **17g**

Bang-Bang Shrimp

This dish features crispy shrimp coated in a sweet and spicy sauce. To evenly coat the shrimp in the sauce, place the shrimp and sauce in a container with a lid and shake it gently. These shrimp are good dipped in ranch dressing.

PREP TIME: **10 minutes**   COOK TIME: **6 minutes**   SERVES: **6**

1/4 cup mayonnaise

1/4 cup Thai sweet chili sauce

1 tablespoon sriracha

2 tablespoons all-purpose flour

1/8 teaspoon kosher salt

1 pound jumbo shrimp, peeled and deveined

2 tablespoons olive oil

1. In a small bowl, stir mayonnaise, sweet chili sauce, and sriracha until combined. Set aside.
2. In a medium bowl, combine flour and salt. Add shrimp and toss to lightly coat shrimp in mixture.
3. Preheat griddle to medium. Add oil and then shrimp to griddle. Cook 2–3 minutes per side until crisp and golden brown. Coat shrimp with prepared sauce and serve.

PER SERVING

Calories: **194**

Fat: **12g**

Protein: **11g**

Sodium: **739mg**

Fiber: **0g**

Carbohydrates: **10g**

Sugar: **7g**

Buffalo Chicken Walking Tacos

This unique version of the traditional walking taco is perfect for tailgating with your griddle. Set up a topping bar with ranch dressing, shredded lettuce, cheese, and jalapeños so everyone can customize their own.

PREP TIME: 10 minutes   **COOK TIME: 10 minutes**   **SERVES: 8**

2 tablespoons olive oil

1 pound ground chicken

1 medium yellow onion, peeled and diced

4 cloves garlic, peeled and minced

$1/2$ teaspoon kosher salt

$1/4$ teaspoon ground black pepper

$1^{1}/4$ cups Buffalo sauce

8 (1.375-ounce) bags corn chips

1. Preheat griddle to medium. Add oil, chicken, onion, garlic, salt, and pepper. Cook, breaking chicken apart with spatulas, for 8 minutes.
2. Pour Buffalo sauce over the mixture and cook 2 more minutes, mixing.
3. Cut top off each bag of chips, lightly crush chips, scoop some Buffalo chicken mixture into each bag, and serve.

PER SERVING

Calories: **325**

Fat: **19g**

Protein: **13g**

Sodium: **1,505mg**

Fiber: **2g**

Carbohydrates: **24g**

Sugar: **1g**

Cheesy Pesto Roll-Ups

The best part of this appetizer is the crispy cheese that forms on the hot surface of the Blackstone. Try a pizza version by swapping out the pesto for pepperoni slices.

PREP TIME: 10 minutes   **COOK TIME: 15 minutes**   **SERVES: 4**

1 (8-ounce, 8-count) tube refrigerated crescent rolls

1/4 cup pesto

4 mozzarella cheese sticks, cut in half crosswise

2 tablespoons unsalted butter, divided

1/3 cup pizza sauce

1. Separate pieces of crescent dough and lay them flat. Put a spoonful of pesto in the center of each and place a piece of cheese over the pesto. Roll up crescent rolls, starting with the larger end, covering over the cheese.

2. Preheat griddle to lowest heat setting. Add 1 tablespoon butter to griddle and, once melted, put filled crescents on griddle. Cover with melting dome or lid for 7 minutes. Flip and cover again for 7–8 more minutes or until golden brown and cooked through.

3. Put remaining 1 tablespoon butter in a small bowl and melt in the microwave for 20–30 seconds. Brush over tops of rolls during the last minute.

4. Serve warm with pizza sauce for dipping.

PER SERVING

Calories: **378**

Fat: **25g**

Protein: **11g**

Sodium: **823mg**

Fiber: **1g**

Carbohydrates: **27g**

Sugar: **7g**

Street Corn Cups

These individual appetizer cups could be a perfect appetizer for a Cinco de Mayo celebration or a nice snack to serve at a taco party. A cup has all the same ingredients as a cob of street corn, but in a form that's much easier (and less messy) to enjoy.

PREP TIME: 15 minutes   **COOK TIME: 10 minutes**   **SERVES: 12**

2 tablespoons vegetable oil

8 ears corn, kernels cut off cobs

1 medium yellow onion, peeled and diced

4 cloves garlic, peeled and minced

$3/4$ teaspoon kosher salt

$1/4$ teaspoon ground black pepper

1 (4-ounce) can diced green chiles

$3/4$ cup mayonnaise

$3/4$ cup sour cream

$1^1/2$ tablespoons chili powder

1 teaspoon paprika

$3/4$ cup crumbled cotija cheese

1. Preheat griddle to medium. Add oil, corn, onion, garlic, salt, pepper. Cook 8 minutes, mixing with spatulas a few times.
2. Add green chiles, mayonnaise, sour cream, chili powder, and paprika. Cook 2 more minutes, mixing. Scoop into cups, top with cheese, and serve.

Serving Tips and Tricks

These have a cool look when served in small, clear plastic cups with spoons. Fill each cup a little more than halfway. It's a nice touch to sprinkle with more chili powder and garnish with fresh chopped cilantro and half of a lime wedge.

PER SERVING

Calories: **233**

Fat: **17g**

Protein: **4g**

Sodium: **389mg**

Fiber: **2g**

Carbohydrates: **16g**

Sugar: **6g**

Chicken Wings

Cooking chicken wings on the griddle creates a crispy skin and juicy, flavorful meat when you bite in. Wings make a great appetizer or game-day snack. Add any seasoning blend or wing sauce of your choice. These are also perfect dipped in ranch dressing.

PREP TIME: 5 minutes   **COOK TIME: 21 minutes**   **SERVES: 6**

3 pounds jumbo, split chicken wings
$3/4$ teaspoon kosher salt
$1/2$ teaspoon ground black pepper
3 tablespoons vegetable oil

Extra-Crispy Chicken Wings

If you prefer your wings extra crispy, you can continue to cook them for a few minutes after removing the melting dome. Raise the heat to medium-high, add extra vegetable oil, and use your tongs to move the chicken wings in the oil, making them as crisp as possible.

1. Season chicken wings with salt and pepper.
2. Preheat griddle to medium-high. Add oil and then chicken wings. Cook 3 minutes per side, using tongs to flip.
3. Lower heat to medium-low. Cover wings with a melting dome or lid. Cook 12–15 more minutes until skin is crispy, removing the dome or lid a few times to flip the wings.
4. Remove from griddle and serve warm.

PER SERVING
Calories: **463**
Fat: **32g**
Protein: **40g**
Sodium: **402mg**
Fiber: **0g**
Carbohydrates: **0g**
Sugar: **0g**

Cheesy Meatball Sliders

Homemade meatballs get the perfect sear when cooked on the Blackstone, and get ready for a showstopping cheese pull when digging into these sliders. You can make the meatballs a day ahead and store them in the refrigerator.

PREP TIME: 15 minutes   **COOK TIME: 11 minutes**   **SERVES: 4**

1 pound 80/20 ground beef

1/2 cup Italian bread crumbs

1/4 cup grated Parmesan cheese

4 cloves garlic, peeled and minced

1 large egg

1 tablespoon Italian seasoning

3/4 teaspoon kosher salt

1/4 teaspoon ground black pepper

1 (12-count) package slider buns, not separated, sliced horizontally to separate tops from bottoms

2 cups shredded mozzarella cheese

2 cups marinara sauce

Meatball Variations

To vary this recipe, you could use ground chicken or turkey in place of the beef; add chopped spinach or fresh herbs to bring some freshness; or try replacing the Parmesan with 1/2 cup ricotta cheese for an extra-tender meatball.

1. In a medium bowl, place beef, bread crumbs, Parmesan, garlic, egg, Italian seasoning, salt, and pepper. Combine with your hands and form 12 meatballs.

2. Preheat griddle to medium. Put meatballs on griddle and cover with melting dome or lid. Cook 8 minutes until cooked through, removing dome a few times to flip them with tongs.

3. Turn heat off and place both bun halves, cut sides down, on griddle for 20 seconds. Turn bottom bun over and add half of mozzarella. Arrange 1 meatball on each bun segment, then top with marinara sauce and remaining mozzarella. Add top bun and cover with dome 1–2 minutes until cheese is melted.

4. Use a large spatula or two regular spatulas to transfer sliders to a tray. Cut and serve.

PER SERVING

Calories: **807**

Fat: **29g**

Protein: **50g**

Sodium: **1,666mg**

Fiber: **6g**

Carbohydrates: **80g**

Sugar: **18g**

Simple Shrimp Cocktail

This classic appetizer has wonderful flavor when prepared on the Blackstone. It's the perfect party food to bring to a gathering, holiday, or party, because it's served cold and easy to transport. This can be made the day before serving.

PREP TIME: 5 minutes   **COOK TIME: 6 minutes**   **SERVES: 8**

2 pounds jumbo shrimp, peeled and deveined (tails on)

$1/2$ teaspoon seafood seasoning

1 tablespoon olive oil

1 medium lemon, cut into 8 wedges

$3/4$ cup cocktail sauce

Peel-and-Eat Shrimp

You can follow this same recipe if you prefer peel-and-eat shrimp—simply leave the shells on the shrimp. Use sharp kitchen scissors to cut the backs of the shells and devein them, or buy the shrimp labeled "easy peel" from the store. Cooking shrimp with the shells on makes them even more flavorful.

1. Pat shrimp dry and place in a medium bowl. Add seafood seasoning and toss to combine.

2. Preheat griddle to medium. Add oil and then shrimp. Cook shrimp 2–3 minutes per side, using tongs to flip, until pink all the way through.

3. During the last minute of cooking, squeeze 2 lemon wedges over shrimp.

4. Refrigerate until ready to serve with cocktail sauce and remaining lemon wedges.

PER SERVING
Calories: **226**
Fat: **2g**
Protein: **15g**

Sodium: **865mg**
Fiber: **0g**
Carbohydrates: **8g**
Sugar: **3g**

Peach and Burrata Crostini

These are sure to impress any guest and create that extra-fancy feeling. The peaches are best if they are just barely ripe, with a slight firmness. Pears can also be used in place of peaches.

PREP TIME: 15 minutes   **COOK TIME: 6 minutes**   **SERVES: 8**

1 (16-ounce) loaf French bread

2 large peaches

2 tablespoons olive oil

$1/2$ teaspoon kosher salt, divided

$1/4$ teaspoon ground black pepper, divided

8 ounces burrata

2 ounces balsamic glaze

6 basil leaves, sliced

1. Cut bread into 16 slices. Cut each peach into 8 slices.
2. Preheat griddle to medium-low. Add oil and then bread slices and peaches. Cook 3 minutes per side. Crostini may be done before peaches, depending on how crisp you prefer them.
3. Sprinkle $1/4$ teaspoon salt and $1/8$ teaspoon pepper on crostini. Assemble by arranging torn burrata on each crostini slice, then topping each with a peach slice. Sprinkle with remaining $1/4$ teaspoon salt and $1/8$ teaspoon pepper.
4. Drizzle balsamic glaze and sprinkle basil on each before serving.

PER SERVING

Calories: **308**

Fat: **11g**

Protein: **12g**

Sodium: **547mg**

Fiber: **2g**

Carbohydrates: **40g**

Sugar: **13g**

Chicken Apple Pigs in a Blanket

This is a special spin on a childhood favorite. You can try many other variations on pigs in a blanket by using different flavors of smoked sausage. Crescent rolls can also be used in place of the puff pastry; you'll just need to take a few minutes off the cooking times.

PREP TIME: 12 minutes   **COOK TIME: 22 minutes**   **SERVES: 4**

1 (12-ounce) sheet puff pastry

1 (12-ounce, 4-count) package smoked chicken apple sausages, cut in half crosswise

1 tablespoon olive oil

1/4 cup Dijon mustard

2 tablespoons pure maple syrup

1. Cut puff pastry sheet into 8 (3-inch-by-4-inch) rectangles. Place a sausage half in the center of each rectangle and then roll it up, overlapping dough slightly, with the ends of the sausage sticking out.

2. Preheat griddle to lowest heat setting. Add oil and then place pigs in a blanket, seam sides down, on griddle. Cover them with a melting dome or lid for 10 minutes.

3. To make dipping sauce, in a small bowl, stir mustard and maple syrup until combined.

4. Flip pigs in a blanket with tongs and cover again for 10–12 more minutes, or until dough is puffed and slightly golden. Serve with dipping sauce.

PER SERVING

Calories: **558**
Fat: **33g**
Protein: **20g**
Sodium: **1,360mg**
Fiber: **2g**
Carbohydrates: **43g**
Sugar: **9g**

Peanut Chicken Wonton Nachos

These crispy wonton chips create an extra-fancy nacho experience. You can find wonton wrappers at most large grocery stores, often in the produce section.

PREP TIME: 10 minutes   **COOK TIME: 14 minutes**   **SERVES: 8**

6 medium scallions

3 tablespoons vegetable oil, divided

1 pound ground chicken

1 cup shredded carrots

1 (8-ounce) bag coleslaw mix

4 cloves garlic, peeled and minced

1/3 cup peanut sauce

1/3 cup hoisin sauce

20 wonton wrappers, cut in half diagonally

2 tablespoons sriracha mayonnaise

1/4 cup chopped roasted peanuts

1. Trim scallions. Finely chop 4 scallions and slice the remaining 2. Set aside separately.
2. Preheat griddle to medium. Add 1 1/2 tablespoons oil and chicken. Cook 3 minutes, breaking chicken apart with spatulas, until cooked through.
3. Add carrots, coleslaw, garlic, and chopped scallions. Mix to combine and cook 6 minutes. Pour peanut and hoisin sauce on top and cook 2 more minutes. Remove and set aside. Scrape griddle clean.
4. Lower heat to medium-low. Add remaining 1 1/2 tablespoons oil and wonton wrappers. Cook 2–3 minutes, flipping wontons a few times and removing them once they are crisped to the level you prefer.
5. Place wonton chips on a plate and top with chicken mixture. Drizzle with sriracha mayonnaise and sprinkle with peanuts and sliced scallions. Serve immediately.

PER SERVING
Calories: **322**
Fat: **15g**
Protein: **16g**
Sodium: **565mg**
Fiber: **4g**
Carbohydrates: **29g**
Sugar: **9g**

Crab-Stuffed Mushrooms

This dish's cheesy seafood filling pairs perfectly with grilled mushrooms. You can also use cooked, chopped shrimp in place of the crab.

PREP TIME: 15 minutes   **COOK TIME: 10 minutes**   **SERVES: 5**

8 ounces cooked crabmeat

8 ounces cream cheese, at room temperature

1 cup shredded Parmesan cheese

1 tablespoon Worcestershire sauce

1 tablespoon lemon juice

2 teaspoons seafood seasoning

1 tablespoon olive oil

20 baby portobello mushrooms, stems removed

1. In a medium bowl, combine crab, cream cheese, Parmesan, Worcestershire sauce, lemon juice, and seafood seasoning.

2. Preheat griddle to medium. Add oil and then mushrooms, stem sides down, and cook 5 minutes. Remove mushrooms from griddle and stuff them with crab filling.

3. Place mushrooms back on Blackstone, stuffed sides up. Cover with melting dome or lid for 5 more minutes. Serve warm.

PER SERVING
Calories: **297**
Fat: **20g**
Protein: **19g**

Sodium: **953mg**
Fiber: **0g**
Carbohydrates: **7g**
Sugar: **3g**

Sriracha Chicken Sliders

Handheld sliders always make fantastic tailgate snacks or game-day appetizers, and these chicken ones are delicious. You can substitute barbecue sauce for the sriracha if desired.

PREP TIME: **10 minutes**   COOK TIME: **10 minutes**   SERVES: **4**

1 pound ground chicken

3 cloves garlic, peeled and minced

3 tablespoons sriracha

1 tablespoon soy sauce

$1/2$ teaspoon kosher salt

2 tablespoons vegetable oil

4 (1-ounce) slices pepper jack cheese, cut in half

8 slider buns

$1/3$ cup mayonnaise

$1/2$ cup chopped cilantro

1. In a medium bowl, place chicken, garlic, sriracha, soy sauce, and salt. Mix with your hands and shape into 8 slider patties.
2. Preheat griddle to medium. Add oil and then patties. Cook 4–5 minutes per side or until cooked through. Right after flipping, add cheese to allow time to melt. Place buns on griddle, cut sides down, for 20 seconds to toast.
3. Place patties on bottom buns and top with mayonnaise and cilantro. Add top buns and serve.

PER SERVING

Calories: **664**

Fat: **40g**

Protein: **37g**

Sodium: **1,319mg**

Fiber: **2g**

Carbohydrates: **40g**

Sugar: **9g**

Taco-Loaded Sweet Potato Fries

These fries make a fun snack or appetizer and, honestly, they can be a snacky weekend dinner too. Don't like sweet potato fries? Simply use regular waffle fries instead. Try topping these with lettuce, sour cream, and pickled red onions for the ultimate experience.

PREP TIME: 5 minutes   **COOK TIME: 15 minutes**   **SERVES: 8**

1 pound 80/20 ground beef

1 (24-ounce) bag frozen sweet potato waffle fries, thawed

3 tablespoons taco seasoning

2 cups shredded Cheddar cheese

1. Preheat griddle to medium. Put beef on one side of the Blackstone. Lay waffle fries in a single layer on the other side.
2. Cook beef 7 minutes, breaking it apart with spatulas as it cooks. Flip fries a few times with tongs.
3. During the last 2 minutes the beef is cooking, add and mix in taco seasoning, along with $1/4$ cup water.
4. Remove meat and continue to cook and flip fries 6–8 more minutes until crispy.
5. Top fries with meat and cheese. Cover with melting dome or lid 1 more minute until cheese is melted and serve.

PER SERVING

Calories: **357**

Fat: **14g**

Protein: **19g**

Sodium: **641mg**

Fiber: **3g**

Carbohydrates: **23g**

Sugar: **7g**

Cheddar Cheese Crisps

This yummy low-carb snack is easily customizable. You can use shredded Parmesan cheese in place of Cheddar if you like, and additions—such as cooked, crumbled bacon; fresh or dried herbs; or thinly sliced jalapeños—can be added right after the cheese hits the griddle.

PREP TIME: **5 minutes**   COOK TIME: **6 minutes**   SERVES: **4**

1 (8-ounce) bag shredded Cheddar cheese

$1/2$ teaspoon paprika

$1/2$ teaspoon garlic powder

Helpful Hints

You may want to cook these in smaller batches if it's your first time, just to keep a better eye on them. Wiggle the spatula to get under the cheese when flipping, as cheese tends to stick to the griddle surface. Store extras in a plastic bag for up to 2 days.

1. In a medium bowl, toss cheese, paprika, and garlic powder until combined.
2. Preheat griddle to medium-low. Place cheese on griddle in 16 equal mounds. Cook 2–3 minutes per side until cheese is melted and bubbly.
3. The cheese will remain soft as long as it's warm, so allow time for these to become completely cool and crispy before serving.

PER SERVING
Calories: **232**
Fat: **17g**
Protein: **14g**
Sodium: **365mg**
Fiber: **0g**
Carbohydrates: **1g**
Sugar: **0g**

Bacon Jalapeño Corn Dip

You will need a large (12-inch) cast iron skillet or a 9-inch-by-13-inch foil pan for this recipe. Have an oven mitt or towel available to handle the hot pan. For a less spicy version, use canned green chiles in place of jalapeños. Serve with tortilla chips or scoop-shaped corn chips for dipping.

PREP TIME: 15 minutes **COOK TIME: 23 minutes** **SERVES: 10**

8 ounces cream cheese, softened

3/4 cup mayonnaise

3/4 cup sour cream

2 cups shredded pepper jack cheese

1 (4-ounce) can diced jalapeño peppers, undrained

3 tablespoons dry ranch seasoning

8 slices bacon

6 ears corn, kernels cut off cobs

1 medium yellow onion, peeled and diced

1/2 teaspoon kosher salt

4 cloves garlic, peeled and minced

1. In a cast iron skillet or foil pan, put cream cheese, mayonnaise, sour cream, pepper jack, jalapeños, and ranch seasoning. Combine and set aside.

2. Preheat griddle to medium-low. Add bacon and cook 5–7 minutes, flipping a few times, until crisp. Remove and set aside; crumble once cool.

3. Scrape most of bacon grease into grease cup and raise heat to medium. Add corn, onion, and salt. Cook 8 minutes, mixing with spatulas a few times. Add garlic and cook 2 more minutes, mixing.

4. Transfer corn mixture to the skillet or pan and add crumbled bacon. Place pan on griddle (scrape griddle clean if needed). Cook 5–6 minutes, stirring a few times, until melted and combined. Serve immediately.

PER SERVING
Calories: **288**
Fat: **25g**
Protein: **6g**

Sodium: **880mg**
Fiber: **1g**
Carbohydrates: **6g**
Sugar: **2g**

Bacon-Wrapped Barbecue Chicken Bites

These are great served warm or at room temperature. For a nice presentation, spear them with decorative toothpicks on a platter and serve with a side of barbecue sauce for dipping.

PREP TIME: 15 minutes   **COOK TIME: 12 minutes**   **SERVES: 6**

1 pound boneless, skinless chicken thighs, cut into 18 pieces

1 tablespoon Worcestershire sauce

1 tablespoon barbecue seasoning, divided

6 slices bacon, cut into thirds crosswise

1. Put chicken in a medium bowl. Add Worcestershire sauce and $1/2$ tablespoon barbecue seasoning; toss until combined.
2. Wrap each piece of chicken in a third of a slice of bacon, stretching bacon if needed and overlapping ends slightly. Sprinkle bacon with remaining $1/2$ tablespoon barbecue seasoning.
3. Place bacon-wrapped chicken pieces on cold griddle, seam sides down. Then turn heat to medium-low and cook 7 minutes. Flip with tongs and cook 4–5 more minutes or until bacon is crisped to your liking. Let cool slightly before serving.

PER SERVING
Calories: **149**
Fat: **8g**
Protein: **17g**

Sodium: **446mg**
Fiber: **0g**
Carbohydrates: **1g**
Sugar: **0g**

Puff Pastry Steak Bites

This upscale-looking appetizer is not as difficult as it may seem. You could include Caramelized Onions and Mushrooms (Chapter 4) in the filling to take it up a notch. Another idea: Add a dollop of creamy cheese and herb spread on top of the steak before wrapping it in the puff pastry.

PREP TIME: 15 minutes   **COOK TIME: 25 minutes**   **SERVES: 4**

2 tablespoons olive oil, divided

1 pound sirloin steak, cut into 12 pieces

1/2 teaspoon kosher salt

1/4 teaspoon ground black pepper

2 tablespoons balsamic vinegar

1 (12-ounce) sheet puff pastry, cut into 12 (3-inch) squares

1/4 cup horseradish sauce

1. Preheat griddle to medium-high. Add 1 tablespoon oil to griddle and then add steak, salt, and pepper. Cook, mixing a few times with spatulas, for 3 minutes. During last minute of cooking time, add vinegar. Remove and set aside. Scrape griddle and turn it off.
2. Once steak is cool, place one piece in the center of each puff pastry square. Fold sides over steak diagonally and press so they are sealed.
3. Preheat griddle to lowest heat setting. Add remaining 1 tablespoon oil to griddle, then add puff pastry bites, seam sides down. Cook for 10 minutes covered with a melting dome or lid.
4. Flip them and cover again for 10–12 more minutes until pastry is puffed and golden.
5. Serve with horseradish sauce for dipping.

PER SERVING

Calories: **597**

Fat: **33g**

Protein: **30g**

Sodium: **616mg**

Fiber: **4g**

Carbohydrates: **36g**

Sugar: **1g**

Pepperoni Pizza Pretzels

This recipe makes a simple snack that is ready in minutes—perfect for game day, movie or game night with the family, or after school as a snack for the kids. You can try mixing these up with whatever other pizza toppings you like.

PREP TIME: 5 minutes   **COOK TIME: 6 minutes**   **SERVES: 6**

2 tablespoons unsalted butter, melted

1 teaspoon Italian seasoning

1/2 teaspoon garlic powder

1/4 teaspoon kosher salt

6 frozen soft pretzels, thawed

2 cups shredded mozzarella cheese

24 regular-sized slices pepperoni

1 cup pizza sauce

1. To a small bowl, add butter, Italian seasoning, garlic powder, and salt. Mix until combined.
2. Preheat griddle to medium-low. Place pretzels, top-side down, on griddle. Cook 3 minutes and then flip.
3. Brush butter mixture over pretzels, then top them with cheese and pepperoni. Cover with melting dome or lid for 2–3 more minutes until cheese is melted.
4. Serve with pizza sauce for dipping.

PER SERVING
Calories: **335**
Fat: **11g**
Protein: **14g**

Sodium: **662mg**
Fiber: **2g**
Carbohydrates: **40g**
Sugar: **3g**

Loaded Potato Chips

These chips are similar to potato skins and can be topped with sour cream or drizzled with ranch if desired. Be sure to cook your bacon on the griddle before the potatoes go on so that the bacon is cool enough to crumble on top before serving.

PREP TIME: 10 minutes   **COOK TIME: 19 minutes**   **SERVES: 6**

5 slices bacon

2 tablespoons olive oil

2 medium russet potatoes, sliced
  $1/4$ inch thick

$1/2$ teaspoon kosher salt

$1/4$ teaspoon ground black pepper

$1^1/2$ cups shredded Colby jack
  cheese

1. Preheat griddle to medium-low. Place bacon on griddle. Cook 5–7 minutes, flipping a few times until cooked to your taste and remove.

2. Turn the heat up to medium. Add oil and then potato slices. Season with salt and pepper. Cook 6 minutes per side.

3. Sprinkle with cheese and crumble bacon on top. Remove from griddle once cheese is melted and serve warm.

PER SERVING

Calories: 241

Fat: **15g**

Protein: **11g**

Sodium: **499mg**

Fiber: **1g**

Carbohydrates: **13g**

Sugar: **1g**

CHAPTER 4

Side Dishes

Often, people tend to concentrate on the protein and don't take the time to fill their plates and bodies with any healthy sides. All the while, the fresh produce you carefully chose at the store or farmers' market waits in the refrigerator until it gets slimy and you inevitably toss it out. Not only is this a waste of healthful food, but it is also a big waste of money. Luckily, the Blackstone griddle is here to save the day (and your meal). With a griddle you can have roasted, seasonal vegetables in minutes while the main dish is being prepared!

In this chapter you'll find a range of easy, delicious sides to go with your main dish. With recipes from Naan and Stir-Fried Ramen Noodles to Brussels Sprouts with Apples and Bacon and Yellow Squash Fritters, you'll be glad you took a few extra minutes to create a delicious side for your meal!

Parmesan Garlic Mushrooms and Zucchini

This is a tasty vegetable combo perfect for hibachi night. These vegetables taste very good dipped in homemade yum-yum sauce (see Shrimp Fried Rice in Chapter 7).

PREP TIME: 10 minutes   **COOK TIME: 11 minutes**   **SERVES: 4**

1 tablespoon olive oil

8 ounces baby portobello mushrooms, sliced

1 medium zucchini, sliced

$1/2$ teaspoon kosher salt

$1/4$ teaspoon ground black pepper

6 cloves garlic, peeled and minced

$1/4$ cup shredded Parmesan cheese

1. Preheat griddle to medium. Add oil and then mushrooms and cook 4 minutes, tossing with spatulas.
2. Add zucchini, salt, and pepper. Cook 4 more minutes, mixing.
3. Add garlic and cook 2–3 more minutes. During the last minute of cooking, sprinkle Parmesan cheese on top.
4. When vegetables reach the tenderness you prefer, remove from griddle and serve.

PER SERVING

Calories: **70**

Fat: **4g**

Protein: **4g**

Sodium: **332mg**

Fiber: **1g**

Carbohydrates: **6g**

Sugar: **2g**

Bacon Cranberry Green Beans

These are easy enough to be a weeknight side dish. Or double the recipe and proudly serve them as a holiday side. Top with crumbled feta cheese and sliced almonds for even more pizzazz.

PREP TIME: 15 minutes   **COOK TIME: 19 minutes**   **SERVES: 4**

4 slices bacon

1 pound green beans, trimmed

$1/4$ teaspoon kosher salt

$1/8$ teaspoon ground black pepper

1 tablespoon unsalted butter

$1/3$ cup dried cranberries

Canned Green Beans

Fresh green beans are best, but sometimes busy weeknights require more simplicity. You can use 2 (14-ounce) cans of green beans, drained, instead of fresh beans in this side dish. After removing the bacon from the griddle, just add your canned beans and cook 2–3 minutes before adding the pepper, butter, cranberries, and bacon. Canned beans often already contain salt, so taste your creation before adding more. No melting dome or lid needed.

1. Preheat griddle to medium-low. Place bacon on griddle and cook 5–7 minutes, flipping a few times. Remove when crisped to your preference and scrape half of the grease off the griddle.

2. Add green beans to griddle. Add a squirt of water and cook 6 minutes under a melting dome or lid. Remove dome or lid a few times during the cooking time to mix beans, adding more water each time before covering again.

3. Cook 5 more minutes without dome or lid, mixing with spatulas. Add salt, pepper, butter, and cranberries and crumble bacon over everything. Mix for 1 more minute and then serve.

PER SERVING

Calories: **135**
Fat: **6g**
Protein: **6g**

Sodium: **320mg**
Fiber: **3g**
Carbohydrates: **16g**
Sugar: **10g**

Crispy Smashed Potatoes

This potato side dish is sure to become a favorite. For a little more zing, add grated Parmesan cheese or rosemary to the garlic butter.

PREP TIME: 20 minutes   **COOK TIME: 9 minutes**   **SERVES: 4**

1 pound petite red potatoes

1 1/2 teaspoons kosher salt, divided

3 tablespoons unsalted butter, melted

4 cloves garlic, peeled and finely minced

1 teaspoon Italian seasoning

3 teaspoons fresh thyme leaves, divided

1 tablespoon olive oil

1/4 teaspoon ground black pepper

1 cup shredded mozzarella cheese

1. Place potatoes and 1 teaspoon salt in a large pot and cover with water. Boil potatoes over high heat 14–16 minutes until tender.

2. In a small bowl, combine butter with garlic, Italian seasoning, and 2 teaspoons thyme leaves. Set aside.

3. Preheat griddle to medium. Add oil and then boiled potatoes, spaced 3 inches apart. Smash potatoes with a burger press or sturdy cup and then season with pepper and remaining 1/2 teaspoon salt.

4. Cook 8 minutes, flipping halfway through the cooking time. Spoon garlic butter and sprinkle cheese over potatoes. Cover with a melting dome or lid for 1 minute until cheese is melted. Garnish with remaining 1 teaspoon thyme leaves and serve.

PER SERVING

Calories: **267**

Fat: **14g**

Protein: **8g**

Sodium: **710mg**

Fiber: **3g**

Carbohydrates: **26g**

Sugar: **2g**

Yellow Squash Fritters

You'll need about one large, or two small, yellow squash for these fritters. If you like, swap in zucchini for some or all of the squash. Either vegetable is easy to shred using a simple box grater.

PREP TIME: 25 minutes*   **COOK TIME: 6 minutes**   **SERVES: 4**

2 cups shredded yellow squash

1 shallot, peeled and finely minced

1 large egg, beaten

1/3 cup panko bread crumbs

1/2 cup all-purpose flour

3 tablespoons grated Parmesan cheese

1/2 tablespoon Cajun seasoning

2 tablespoons olive oil

Dipping Sauce Options

You can mix sour cream and chopped chives for an easy dipping sauce for these fritters. Another option is to combine mayonnaise, a little Cajun seasoning, and a few dashes of hot sauce. To go a little fancier, try combining plain Greek yogurt with lemon juice and feta cheese crumbles.

1. Allow squash to drain on a layer of paper towels for 5 minutes. Then transfer to a new layer of paper towels, wrap towels around squash, and squeeze to remove any excess liquid.

2. Place squash in a large bowl and add shallots, egg, panko, flour, cheese, and Cajun seasoning. Mix until combined. Let sit 10 minutes and then use your hands to divide and shape batter into 8 balls.

3. Preheat griddle to medium. Add oil, put fritters on griddle, and flatten them slightly with spatulas.

4. Cook 2–3 minutes per side until golden brown. Serve warm.

*Includes resting time.

PER SERVING
Calories: **180**
Fat: **7g**
Protein: **6g**

Sodium: **135mg**
Fiber: **1g**
Carbohydrates: **22g**
Sugar: **2g**

Corn on the Cob

This corn is one of the easiest sides to make at the same time as your main dish. This recipe shows you how to make the simplest version; jazz it up by adding a seasoning blend or brushing on some plain or seasoned melted butter to complement your meal.

PREP TIME: 5 minutes **COOK TIME: 11 minutes** **SERVES: 4**

4 ears corn, shucked

2 tablespoons olive oil

1/2 teaspoon kosher salt

1/4 teaspoon ground black pepper

PER SERVING
Calories: **147**
Fat: **8g**
Protein: **3g**
Sodium: **255mg**
Fiber: **2g**
Carbohydrates: **19g**
Sugar: **6g**

1. Brush corn with oil and season all sides with salt and pepper.
2. Preheat griddle to medium. Place corn on Blackstone and cover with melting dome or lid.
3. Cook 9–11 minutes, removing the dome a few times to turn corn with tongs. Cook until corn is as tender and charred as you like. Serve warm.

Garlic Parmesan Asparagus

The Blackstone's even, dry heat helps asparagus keep its vibrant green color. This dish's simple seasonings make it a nice match for nearly any entrée. You can substitute mozzarella cheese for the Parmesan if preferred.

PREP TIME: 5 minutes **COOK TIME: 10 minutes** **SERVES: 4**

1 tablespoon unsalted butter

1 pound asparagus, trimmed

1/4 teaspoon kosher salt

1/4 teaspoon garlic powder

1/4 cup shredded Parmesan cheese

PER SERVING
Calories: **52**
Fat: **3g**
Protein: **3g**
Sodium: **206mg**
Fiber: **1g**
Carbohydrates: **3g**
Sugar: **1g**

1. Preheat griddle to medium. Add butter and, once melted, asparagus, salt, and garlic powder.
2. Cook 8–10 minutes until tender, turning the asparagus a few times with tongs.
3. During the last minute of cooking, sprinkle with cheese. Serve warm.

Naan

Naan is a type of Indian flatbread usually cooked in a clay oven called a tandoor. Traditionally, people tear off pieces of naan to scoop and eat the meat or vegetable dishes served alongside it. On the Blackstone, naan is so easy to cook, it can also make a convenient homemade base for pizzalike creations (Chapter 5), or even for tacos (Chapters 6 and 8). You can work and knead the dough by hand if you don't have a stand mixer.

PREP TIME: 2 hours, 25 minutes*   **COOK TIME: 2 minutes**   **SERVES: 6**

$1/4$ cup warm water

$1^1/2$ teaspoons active dry yeast

1 tablespoon granulated sugar, divided

1 large egg yolk

$1/3$ cup 2% milk

$1/3$ cup full-fat plain Greek yogurt

2 tablespoons olive oil

$3/4$ teaspoon kosher salt

$2^1/3$ cups all-purpose flour, divided

Naan Variations

To add more flavor to your naan, make garlic butter to brush onto it right after cooking. Fresh herbs would also be a nice addition to the butter—or brush the naan with plain butter and add a sprinkle of sesame seeds, poppy seeds, or everything bagel seasoning.

1. To a small bowl, add water, yeast, and $1/8$ teaspoon sugar. Stir and let sit 10 minutes until bubbly.
2. To the bowl of a stand mixer, add yeast mixture, remaining sugar, egg yolk, milk, yogurt, oil, salt, and half of flour. Mix with paddle attachment on low for 1 minute.
3. Change to hook attachment, add remaining flour, and mix on low for 2 minutes. Dough should easily pull away from sides of bowl.
4. Spray a large bowl with nonstick spray and transfer dough to bowl. Cover with a kitchen towel and let rest 2 hours.
5. Punch dough down and cut into 6 portions. On a lightly floured surface, roll each portion into a $1/4$-inch-thick oval.
6. Preheat griddle to medium. Sprinkle about 1 tablespoon water onto dough ovals and place all 6 ovals on griddle, wet sides down. Cook 35–45 seconds per side until golden brown and bubbly. Serve warm.

PER SERVING

Calories: **255**

Fat: **6g**

Protein: **7g**

Sodium: **254mg**

Fiber: **2g**

Carbohydrates: **41g**

Sugar: **3g**

*Includes resting time.

Cheesy Garlic Zucchini

This flavorful griddle side dish cooks well alongside almost any main dish on your griddle. Cook some chicken or steak at the same time for a complete Blackstone meal. To add to the flavor party, try dipping the zucchini in ranch dressing.

PREP TIME: 10 minutes   **COOK TIME: 6 minutes**   **SERVES: 4**

2 medium zucchini, ends cut off

3 tablespoons olive oil, divided

$1/2$ teaspoon garlic and herb seasoning

1 cup shredded mozzarella cheese

1. Slice each zucchini into $1/4$-inch pieces, either lengthwise into strips or crosswise into circles. For even slicing, use a mandoline or a sharp knife.
2. Use 1 tablespoon oil to brush both sides of each zucchini slice. Sprinkle with garlic and herb seasoning.
3. Preheat griddle to medium. Add remaining 2 tablespoons oil and then zucchini slices.
4. Cook zucchini 2–3 minutes per side until tender. During the last minute of cooking time, sprinkle with cheese. Nudge some cheese off edges of zucchini and onto griddle to create some crispy cheese edges. Serve warm.

PER SERVING

Calories: **156**

Fat: **12g**

Protein: **6g**

Sodium: **199mg**

Fiber: **1g**

Carbohydrates: **5g**

Sugar: **3g**

Teriyaki Broccolini

Broccolini is a vegetable similar to broccoli. The florets are smaller, and the stalks are thinner and more tender. It has a slightly sweet flavor compared to broccoli and is high in vitamins C and K and other antioxidants.

PREP TIME: 5 minutes   **COOK TIME: 10 minutes**   **SERVES: 4**

1 tablespoon olive oil

1 pound broccolini

1/4 teaspoon kosher salt

2 cloves garlic, peeled and minced

2 tablespoons teriyaki sauce

1/2 tablespoon soy sauce

1/2 tablespoon white sesame seeds

1. Preheat griddle to medium-low. Add oil, broccolini, and salt. Cook 6 minutes, flipping a few times with tongs.
2. Add garlic, teriyaki sauce, and soy sauce. Cook 3–4 more minutes until tender, flipping a few times during cooking. Garnish with sesame seeds before serving.

PER SERVING
Calories: **70**
Fat: **3g**
Protein: **4g**

Sodium: **604mg**
Fiber: **3g**
Carbohydrates: **8g**
Sugar: **3g**

Acorn Squash Halves

Making this dish is a sweet way to celebrate fall—or to bring on that cozy fall feeling any time of year. You can replace the brown sugar with maple syrup if you prefer. Pumpkin or apple pie seasoning would also be a nice addition.

PREP TIME: **10 minutes** COOK TIME: **10 minutes** SERVES: **4**

2 medium acorn squash

2 tablespoons olive oil

1/2 teaspoon kosher salt

1/4 teaspoon ground black pepper

4 tablespoons unsalted butter

4 tablespoons light brown sugar

1. Poke a few holes in each squash with the tip of a sharp knife. Put them in the microwave for 5 minutes.
2. Cut each squash in half, scoop out seeds and pulp, drizzle oil over the cut sides, and season with salt and pepper.
3. Preheat griddle to medium. Place squash halves, cut sides down, on griddle. Squirt squash with some water and cover with a melting dome or lid for 5 minutes. Add more water a few times during the cooking time.
4. Flip squash cut-side up, add more water, and cover to cook for another 5–6 minutes until tender. Divide butter and brown sugar evenly among centers of squash halves. Once butter and sugar have melted, remove squash from griddle and serve with spoons.

PER SERVING
Calories: **299**
Fat: **17g**
Protein: **2g**
Sodium: **251mg**
Fiber: **3g**
Carbohydrates: **36g**
Sugar: **13g**

Caramelized Onions and Mushrooms

Slow and steady wins the race is the theme with this recipe. It takes time to properly caramelize, and it's well worth the wait—an incredible side dish to serve with steak!

PREP TIME: 15 minutes   **COOK TIME: 23 minutes**   **SERVES: 4**

1 tablespoon olive oil

3 medium yellow onions, peeled and thinly sliced

8 ounces white mushrooms, thinly sliced

1/4 teaspoon kosher salt

1/8 teaspoon ground black pepper

2 tablespoons unsalted butter

1 tablespoon balsamic vinegar

1/2 teaspoon light brown sugar

1. Preheat griddle to medium-low. Add oil, onions, mushrooms, salt, and pepper. Cook 18 minutes, mixing a few times. Lower heat if onions start browning too quickly.
2. Add butter, vinegar, and brown sugar. Cook 4–5 more minutes, mixing with spatulas. When done, onions should be soft, with a caramel color. Serve warm.

PER SERVING
Calories: **123**
Fat: **8g**
Protein: **3g**

Sodium: **127mg**
Fiber: **2g**
Carbohydrates: **11g**
Sugar: **6g**

Creamy Lemon Kale

Kale is an excellent source of many vitamins and minerals, as well as fiber, making it one of the top superfoods for your body. This is a very quick low-carb side dish.

PREP TIME: 10 minutes **COOK TIME: 9 minutes** **SERVES: 4**

1 tablespoon olive oil

1 medium yellow onion, peeled and diced

1 (16-ounce) bunch kale, stems removed, chopped

5 cloves garlic, peeled and minced

1/4 teaspoon kosher salt

1/8 teaspoon ground black pepper

2 tablespoons lemon juice

1/4 cup heavy cream

1/4 cup shredded Parmesan cheese

1. Preheat griddle to medium. Add oil and then onion. Cook 3 minutes, mixing with spatulas.
2. Add kale, garlic, salt, and pepper. Cook 3 more minutes, stirring.
3. Add lemon juice, cream, and cheese. Cook another 2–3 minutes, mixing with spatulas a few times until kale is tender and cream has thickened. Serve warm.

PER SERVING
Calories: **160**
Fat: **10g**
Protein: **7g**
Sodium: **249mg**
Fiber: **4g**
Carbohydrates: **14g**
Sugar: **4g**

Stir-Fried Ramen Noodles

These noodles make a quick side dish on the Blackstone, or you can add chicken or shrimp and some vegetables of choice for a complete stir-fried dinner. A drizzle of sriracha, yum-yum sauce, or sesame seeds will add even more deliciousness.

PREP TIME: 15 minutes   **COOK TIME: 12 minutes**   **SERVES: 4**

3 (3-ounce) packages ramen noodles, noodles only (no flavor packet)

1 tablespoon vegetable oil

1 medium yellow onion, peeled and diced

6 cloves garlic, peeled and minced

2 tablespoons hoisin sauce

2 tablespoons soy sauce

4 tablespoons unsalted butter

2 large eggs

4 medium scallions, sliced

Steaming the Noodles

You can choose to cook the noodles right on the Blackstone. Place the bricks of uncooked ramen on the griddle set to medium heat, squirt some water on them, and cover them with a melting dome. Check after a minute, mix them around, and add more water before covering again. Repeat until noodles are cooked to your liking.

1. Bring a large pot filled with water to a boil over high heat. Place noodles in pot and allow to boil for 2 minutes. Drain and rinse well with cold water.

2. Preheat griddle to medium. Add oil, then onion, and cook 3 minutes.

3. Add noodles, garlic, hoisin sauce, soy sauce, and butter and crack in eggs. Cook 7 minutes, tossing with spatulas and breaking apart eggs.

4. Add scallions and cook 1–2 more minutes until noodles are crisped to your liking. Serve warm.

PER SERVING
Calories: **346**
Fat: **21g**
Protein: **9g**
Sodium: **796mg**
Fiber: **2g**
Carbohydrates: **29g**
Sugar: **4g**

Green Beans and Peppers

This is a fresh and colorful vegetable side filled with vitamins A, C, and K and other antioxidants. Sprinkle on a seasoning blend of choice to add your own flavor and pizzazz.

PREP TIME: **15 minutes**   COOK TIME: **12 minutes**   SERVES: **4**

2 tablespoons olive oil

1 pound green beans, trimmed

2 medium red bell peppers, seeded and sliced

1/2 teaspoon kosher salt

1/4 teaspoon ground black pepper

4 cloves garlic, peeled and minced

1 tablespoon unsalted butter, cut into small cubes

1. Preheat griddle to medium. Add oil, green beans, red peppers, salt, and black pepper. Cook 6 minutes under a melting dome or lid. Uncover a few times to stir.

2. Add garlic and butter. Cook uncovered for 5–6 more minutes until vegetables are tender, mixing a few times. Serve.

PER SERVING
Calories: **124**
Fat: **8g**
Protein: **3g**

Sodium: **249mg**
Fiber: **4g**
Carbohydrates: **12g**
Sugar: **6g**

Rosemary Fingerling Potatoes

Fingerling potatoes have a rich, buttery taste, and they come in a gorgeous variety of colors, from gold to red to purple. Rosemary complements the potatoes nicely, but fresh thyme or an Italian seasoning blend would work too.

PREP TIME: 10 minutes   **COOK TIME: 14 minutes**   **SERVES: 4**

3 tablespoons unsalted butter, divided

1 pound fingerling potatoes, sliced in half lengthwise

1/2 teaspoon kosher salt

1/4 teaspoon ground black pepper

4 cloves garlic, peeled and minced

1 tablespoon chopped, fresh rosemary

Adding Water for Potatoes

The purpose of adding water under the melting dome when cooking potatoes is to steam them. Steam cooks food faster than dry air. By adding water and trapping it under the dome, you shorten the total cooking time. That way, the potatoes have a chance to cook all the way through before the outsides become burned.

1. Preheat griddle to medium. Add 1 tablespoon butter and potatoes. Squirt with 3 tablespoons water, cover with melting dome or lid, and cook 10 minutes. Remove dome a few times to flip potatoes, adding 3 more tablespoons water each time before covering again.

2. Set dome aside and add remaining 2 tablespoons butter, salt, pepper, garlic, and rosemary. Cook 3–4 more minutes until potatoes are tender, tossing a few times during cooking. Serve warm.

PER SERVING
Calories: **146**
Fat: **7g**
Protein: **2g**

Sodium: **259mg**
Fiber: **3g**
Carbohydrates: **19g**
Sugar: **1g**

Corn Bread Cakes

This is a tried-and-true recipe for homemade honey corn bread. If you are short on time, you can use a box of corn bread mix and cook it on the Blackstone using these same instructions. Depending on how many egg rings you have, you may need to cook these in batches.

PREP TIME: 15 minutes   **COOK TIME: 16 minutes**   **SERVES: 8**

1 cup yellow cornmeal

1 cup all-purpose flour

$1/3$ cup granulated sugar

2 teaspoons baking powder

$1/2$ teaspoon baking soda

$1/8$ teaspoon kosher salt

$1^{1}/2$ cups 1% buttermilk

2 large eggs

3 tablespoons unsalted butter, melted

1 (14.75-ounce) can cream-style corn

$1/2$ cup honey

1. In a large bowl, whisk cornmeal, flour, sugar, baking powder, baking soda, and salt until combined.
2. Add buttermilk, eggs, butter, corn, and honey. Stir until combined.
3. Preheat griddle to lowest heat setting. Place 16 silicone egg rings on Blackstone and spray them well with nonstick spray. Fill each egg ring $3/4$ full of batter. Cover with melting dome or lid and cook 14–16 minutes or until corn bread is set.
4. Remove cakes from egg rings before serving.

Corn Bread Variations

Feel free to omit the honey for a less sweet corn bread. Also, including some diced jalapeños, shredded cheese of choice, cooked and crumbled bacon, or freshly chopped herbs are all fantastic ways to add variety to this recipe.

PER SERVING

Calories: **321**

Fat: **6g**

Protein: **7g**

Sodium: **478mg**

Fiber: **2g**

Carbohydrates: **62g**

Sugar: **30g**

Maple-Glazed Carrots

A sweet glaze pairs so nicely with carrots. This side dish is perfect with a main dish of pork or chicken. Fresh thyme or a seasoning blend of choice—best added at the same time as the maple syrup—would be a tasty addition to these carrots.

PREP TIME: **5 minutes**   COOK TIME: **13 minutes**   SERVES: **4**

3 tablespoons unsalted butter, divided

1 (16-ounce) bag peeled baby carrots

$1/2$ teaspoon kosher salt

$1/4$ teaspoon ground black pepper

3 tablespoons pure maple syrup

1 tablespoon light brown sugar

1. Preheat griddle to medium. Add 1 tablespoon butter, carrots, and 2 tablespoons water. Cover with melting dome or lid for 8 minutes, removing dome a few times to toss carrots and add 2 more tablespoons water before covering again.

2. Set dome aside and add remaining 2 tablespoons butter, salt, pepper, maple syrup, and brown sugar. Cook 4–5 more minutes until carrots are tender, mixing a few times. Serve.

PER SERVING
Calories: **162**
Fat: **7g**
Protein: **1g**

Sodium: **321mg**
Fiber: **3g**
Carbohydrates: **24g**
Sugar: **18g**

Creamy Corn and Zucchini

This beloved side dish has everything: It's sweet, salty, and creamy, and it's made to showcase summer produce. It's extra-spectacular when made with fresh corn and garden zucchini.

PREP TIME: 15 minutes   **COOK TIME: 12 minutes**   **SERVES: 6**

2 tablespoons olive oil

4 ears corn, kernels cut off cobs

4 cups diced zucchini

3/4 teaspoon kosher salt

1/4 teaspoon ground black pepper

4 cloves garlic, peeled and minced

1 cup heavy cream

1 cup shredded Parmesan cheese

1. Preheat griddle to medium. Add oil, corn, zucchini, salt, and pepper. Cook 6 minutes, mixing a few times with spatulas.
2. Add garlic and cook and stir 3 more minutes.
3. Pour on cream and sprinkle with cheese, using your spatulas to contain the cream at first. Cook 2–3 more minutes until cream thickens and then serve.

PER SERVING

Calories: **297**

Fat: **22g**

Protein: **9g**

Sodium: **498mg**

Fiber: **2g**

Carbohydrates: **18g**

Sugar: **8g**

Brussels Sprouts with Apples and Bacon

This fabulous fall side dish can be doubled to serve at holidays. Dried cranberries and goat cheese added before serving are a nice complement to the sweet and savory flavor combo.

PREP TIME: 15 minutes   **COOK TIME: 12 minutes**   **SERVES: 4**

4 slices bacon, cut into bite-sized pieces

1 medium yellow onion, peeled and diced

1 pound Brussels sprouts, thinly sliced

1 medium Honeycrisp apple (with peel), cored and diced

$1/4$ teaspoon kosher salt

$1/8$ teaspoon ground black pepper

$1/8$ teaspoon crushed red pepper flakes

2 tablespoons honey

$1/4$ cup dried cranberries

$1/4$ cup crumbled goat cheese

1. Preheat griddle to medium. Add bacon and onion and cook 4 minutes, mixing with spatulas a few times.
2. Add Brussels sprouts, apple, salt, black pepper, and red pepper flakes. Cook 6–7 more minutes, tossing a few times until tender.
3. Add honey and cranberries and cook 1 more minute. Remove from griddle, top with cheese, and serve warm.

PER SERVING
Calories: **262**
Fat: **11g**
Protein: **12g**
Sodium: **429mg**
Fiber: **5g**
Carbohydrates: **31g**
Sugar: **21g**

Riced Cilantro Lime Sweet Potatoes

Here is a rice-style dish that's packed with fiber, vitamins, and antioxidants. You may need to pulse the potatoes in two batches, depending on your food processor size. Serve this dish as a side, or make it a meal by topping with taco meat, cheese, and sour cream.

PREP TIME: 15 minutes   **COOK TIME: 8 minutes**   **SERVES: 4**

4 medium sweet potatoes, peeled and cut into 1-inch cubes

2 tablespoons olive oil

1 teaspoon chili powder

1 teaspoon garlic powder

3/4 teaspoon ground cumin

3/4 teaspoon kosher salt

1/2 teaspoon ground black pepper

1/2 cup chopped cilantro

2 tablespoons lime juice

1. Place sweet potato cubes in a food processor and pulse a few times until they have a rice-like consistency.
2. Preheat griddle to medium. Add oil, sweet potatoes, chili powder, garlic powder, cumin, salt, and pepper. Cook 6–7 minutes until soft, flipping with spatulas a few times.
3. Add cilantro and lime juice and mix 1 more minute before serving.

PER SERVING

Calories: **155**

Fat: **5g**

Protein: **3g**

Sodium: **422mg**

Fiber: **4g**

Carbohydrates: **26g**

Sugar: **8g**

CHAPTER 5

Chicken Main Dishes

Chicken often gets a bad rap as bland and uninspired, but it doesn't have to be boring. Ideas for chicken on the Blackstone griddle are endless, so in this chapter you'll find chicken dinner recipes ranging from extra-simple to extraordinary. Some are complete meals in themselves, and some work best paired with a side dish from Chapter 4.

Whether you are craving Chicken Fried Rice, Street Corn Chicken Tacos, Lemon Feta Chicken Kebabs, Peanut Chicken Lettuce Wraps, or Chicken Caesar Tortellini Salads, this chapter has a chicken dish for almost any occasion. Your new favorite chicken dish is here and ready to be served up in minutes!

Chicken Fried Rice

It seems fried rice is one of the dishes that every new Blackstone owner is excited to try. Making the rice a day in advance and storing it, covered, in the refrigerator helps create a crispy rice texture just like in a hibachi-style restaurant.

PREP TIME: 15 minutes   **COOK TIME: 12 minutes**   **SERVES: 6**

2 tablespoons vegetable oil

6 cups cooked, cooled jasmine rice

1 medium yellow onion, peeled and diced

3 large eggs

1 (12-ounce) bag frozen diced peas and carrots, thawed

$1/2$ cup soy sauce, divided

3 tablespoons unsalted butter

4 cloves garlic, peeled and minced

$1^1/2$ pounds boneless, skinless chicken breasts, cut into bite-sized pieces

1 tablespoon lemon juice

$1/2$ tablespoon white sesame seeds

$1/2$ cup yum-yum sauce

1. Preheat griddle to medium-high. Add oil, rice, onion, and eggs. Cook 3 minutes, mixing with spatulas and breaking eggs apart.

2. Add peas and carrots, most of soy sauce (reserve 2 tablespoons), butter, and garlic to rice. Add chicken and remaining soy sauce to a spot on the Blackstone next to rice. Cook both mixtures 6 minutes, mixing each a few times with spatulas.

3. Combine chicken and rice, along with lemon juice and sesame seeds, with spatulas. Cook 2–3 more minutes until rice is as crisp as you like. Serve right away with yum-yum sauce.

Tip for Transferring Rice

You may want to purchase a large scoop to use with your Blackstone. It has sides that prevent food from falling off and is perfect for transferring stir-fries, fried rice, pasta dishes, and sliders from the flat top surface to a tray or platter.

PER SERVING

Calories: **549**

Fat: **25g**

Protein: **29g**

Sodium: **1,400mg**

Fiber: **4g**

Carbohydrates: **55g**

Sugar: **5g**

Thai Basil Chicken

Thai basil is available in larger or specialty grocery stores. If you can't find it, use Italian, holy, or lemon basil instead; the flavor will be slightly different but still tasty. Try topping this dish with fried eggs and sriracha for the ultimate experience.

PREP TIME: 20 minutes   **COOK TIME: 11 minutes**   **SERVES: 4**

2 cups jasmine rice

1 tablespoon vegetable oil

1 medium yellow onion, peeled and diced

1 cup shredded carrots

3 red chili peppers, sliced

1 pound ground chicken

4 cloves garlic, peeled and minced

$1/4$ cup oyster sauce

1 tablespoon soy sauce

20 Thai basil leaves

1. Prepare rice according to package instructions.
2. Preheat griddle to medium. Add oil, onion, carrots, and peppers. Cook 3 minutes, tossing with spatulas.
3. Add chicken, garlic, oyster sauce, and soy sauce. Cook 6 more minutes, breaking chicken apart with spatulas.
4. Add Thai basil and stir 1–2 more minutes until basil leaves are slightly wilted. Serve over rice.

PER SERVING

Calories: **314**

Fat: **11g**

Protein: **22g**

Sodium: **792mg**

Fiber: **3g**

Carbohydrates: **32g**

Sugar: **4g**

Buffalo Chicken Sloppy Joes

Sloppy joes get a fun makeover in this griddle recipe. Think of this as a combo of two favorite dinners: Buffalo wings and the classic messy sandwich we all know and love. For more sophisticated palates, try adding some crumbled blue cheese on top.

PREP TIME: **5 minutes**   COOK TIME: **10 minutes**   SERVES: **4**

1 tablespoon olive oil

1 pound ground chicken

1 medium yellow onion, peeled and diced

3 cloves garlic, peeled and minced

$1/2$ teaspoon kosher salt

$1/4$ teaspoon ground black pepper

1 (12-ounce) can petite diced tomatoes, drained

1 cup Buffalo sauce

4 hamburger buns

$1/2$ cup ranch dressing

1. Preheat griddle to medium. Add oil, chicken, onion, garlic, salt, and pepper. Cook 5 minutes, breaking chicken apart with spatulas as it cooks.
2. Add tomatoes and Buffalo sauce. Cook 4–5 more minutes until thickened, mixing a few times.
3. Serve on hamburger buns with ranch dressing.

PER SERVING
Calories: **324**
Fat: **12g**
Protein: **23g**
Sodium: **2,506mg**
Fiber: **3g**
Carbohydrates: **28g**
Sugar: **6g**

Garlic Herb Chicken and Potatoes

You can use any of your favorite seasoning blends—try barbecue, Caribbean, or taco seasoning—in place of the garlic and herb seasoning in this recipe.

PREP TIME: 15 minutes   **COOK TIME: 16 minutes**   **SERVES: 4**

2 tablespoons olive oil, divided

1$\frac{1}{2}$ pounds red potatoes, diced

1$\frac{1}{2}$ pounds boneless, skinless chicken thighs, cut into bite-sized pieces

4 cloves garlic, peeled and minced

2 tablespoons garlic herb seasoning

1. Preheat griddle to medium. Add 1 tablespoon oil and then add potatoes. Squirt potatoes with 3 tablespoons water. Cover with melting dome or lid for 7 minutes. Stir potatoes and add 3 more tablespoons water and re-cover a few times.

2. Set dome aside and add remaining 1 tablespoon oil, chicken, minced garlic, and garlic herb seasoning. Cook and stir with spatulas 8–9 more minutes until potatoes are tender and chicken is cooked through. Serve.

PER SERVING

Calories: **419**

Fat: **13g**

Protein: **33g**

Sodium: **143mg**

Fiber: **4g**

Carbohydrates: **38g**

Sugar: **3g**

Chicken Bacon Ranch Flatbreads

Chicken, bacon, and ranch may become your three best friends—they just play well together. This recipe uses precooked naan, making this a very quick meal to prepare.

PREP TIME: 5 minutes   **COOK TIME: 6 minutes**   **SERVES: 2**

2 (4-ounce) pieces naan

$\frac{1}{2}$ cup ranch dressing

1 cup cooked, chopped chicken

4 slices bacon, cooked and crumbled

2 cups shredded mozzarella cheese

1. Preheat griddle to medium-low. Place naan pieces on Blackstone. After 1 minute, flip them over and add ranch dressing, chicken, bacon, and cheese.

2. Cover with a melting dome or lid until cheese is melted, about 3–5 minutes, and then serve.

PER SERVING

Calories: **846**

Fat: **35g**

Protein: **61g**

Sodium: **1,951mg**

Fiber: **2g**

Carbohydrates: **63g**

Sugar: **8g**

Chicken Fajita Tortellini

This dish has all the flavors of fajitas, but with an Italian twist. Tortellini on the griddle has a unique texture: slightly crisp on the outside, but still soft and creamy on the inside.

PREP TIME: 15 minutes   **COOK TIME: 16 minutes**   **SERVES: 6**

1 (20-ounce) bag frozen cheese tortellini, thawed

2 tablespoons vegetable oil

1 medium yellow onion, peeled and sliced

1 medium red bell pepper, seeded and sliced

1 medium green bell pepper, seeded and sliced

1 1/2 pounds boneless, skinless chicken thighs, cut into bite-sized pieces

6 cloves garlic, peeled and minced

2 tablespoons fajita seasoning

3/4 teaspoon kosher salt

1 cup salsa

1 1/2 cups heavy cream

1 1/2 cups shredded Cheddar cheese

1 medium jalapeño pepper, seeded and sliced

1. Preheat griddle to medium. Add tortellini, squirt some water on top, and cover with a melting dome or lid. Cook 3 minutes. Halfway through cooking time, remove lid to stir and add more water before covering again.

2. Set dome aside and add oil, onion, peppers, chicken, garlic, fajita seasoning, and salt. Cook 10 minutes, mixing with spatulas.

3. Add salsa, cream, and cheese. Cook 2–3 more minutes, stirring constantly, until cream thickens into a sauce. Serve with sliced jalapeño on top.

PER SERVING

Calories: **723**

Fat: **42g**

Protein: **37g**

Sodium: **1,249mg**

Fiber: **8g**

Carbohydrates: **45g**

Sugar: **7g**

Teriyaki Chicken Egg Roll in a Bowl

This recipe gives you all the yummy insides of an egg roll, but without the heavy, deep-fried wrapper. Use a teriyaki sauce with no high fructose corn syrup or added sugar for a healthier, low-carb version.

PREP TIME: 10 minutes   **COOK TIME: 10 minutes**   **SERVES: 4**

1 tablespoon vegetable oil

1 pound ground chicken

1 (8-ounce) bag coleslaw mix

1 cup shredded carrots

4 medium scallions, sliced

5 cloves garlic, peeled and minced

2/3 cup teriyaki sauce

1/4 cup sriracha mayonnaise

1/4 cup chopped roasted peanuts

1. Preheat griddle to medium. Add oil and chicken. Cook 3 minutes, breaking chicken apart with spatulas.

2. Add coleslaw, carrots, scallions, and garlic. Stir and cook for 5 more minutes.

3. Add teriyaki sauce. Stir and cook 1–2 more minutes until sauce is thickened.

4. Serve in bowls, drizzled with sriracha mayonnaise and topped with peanuts.

PER SERVING

Calories: **423**

Fat: **24g**

Protein: **26g**

Sodium: **2,168mg**

Fiber: **6g**

Carbohydrates: **26g**

Sugar: **16g**

Lazy Chicken Enchiladas

This recipe delivers on the promise of "lazy." Compared with the usual process of rolling and baking enchiladas, it is very quick and easy to make, and it still has all the familiar flavors.

PREP TIME: 10 minutes   **COOK TIME: 10 minutes**   **SERVES: 6**

2 tablespoons vegetable oil, divided

1 pound boneless, skinless chicken breasts, cut into bite-sized pieces

1/2 teaspoon kosher salt

8 (5-inch) corn tortillas, cut into 1-inch strips

1 (14-ounce) can corn, drained

1 (14-ounce) can black beans, drained and rinsed

1 (4-ounce) can green chiles

2 (10-ounce) cans green enchilada sauce

1/2 cup sour cream

2 cups shredded Cheddar cheese

1. Preheat griddle to medium. Add 1 tablespoon oil, then chicken and salt. Cook 5 minutes, stirring with spatulas.

2. Add remaining 1 tablespoon oil, tortillas, corn, beans, green chiles, enchilada sauce, and sour cream. Mix together with spatulas a few times and cook 4 more minutes.

3. Sprinkle with cheese and cover with melting dome or lid for 1 more minute. Serve once cheese is melted.

PER SERVING
Calories: **514**
Fat: **24g**
Protein: **33g**
Sodium: **1,174mg**
Fiber: **8g**
Carbohydrates: **40g**
Sugar: **4g**

Peanut Chicken Lettuce Wraps

For a creative taco treat, you could serve this same peanut chicken filling in warm flour tortillas. Alternatively, try it over cooked jasmine rice. However you serve it, you can take a shortcut by using store-bought peanut sauce for a really quick meal.

PREP TIME: 20 minutes   **COOK TIME: 10 minutes**   **SERVES: 4**

1/4 cup hoisin sauce

1/4 cup peanut butter

2 tablespoons soy sauce

1 tablespoon honey

3 cloves garlic, peeled and minced

1 teaspoon grated ginger

1 tablespoon vegetable oil

1 medium yellow onion, peeled and diced

1 medium red bell pepper, seeded and diced

1 cup shredded carrots

1 pound ground chicken

1 head Boston lettuce, leaves separated

1/4 cup chopped roasted peanuts

1. To make sauce, in a medium bowl, add hoisin sauce, peanut butter, soy sauce, honey, garlic, and ginger. Whisk until combined.

2. Preheat griddle to medium. Add oil, onion, pepper, and carrots. Cook 3 minutes, stirring a few times with spatulas.

3. Add chicken and sauce and cook 7 minutes, mixing and breaking chicken apart with spatulas.

4. Let mixture cool slightly. Serve in lettuce wraps, topped with peanuts.

PER SERVING
Calories: **416**
Fat: **23g**
Protein: **27g**
Sodium: **778mg**
Fiber: **5g**
Carbohydrates: **24g**
Sugar: **14g**

Creamy Spinach and Artichoke Chicken

This recipe was inspired by spinach and artichoke dip. It has the same creamy, cheesy taste as the dip, but it's a complete Blackstone dinner. Chicken breasts can be used in place of the chicken thighs if preferred.

PREP TIME: **20 minutes**   COOK TIME: **10 minutes**   SERVES: **4**

2 tablespoons olive oil

$1^1/_2$ pounds boneless, skinless chicken thighs, cut into bite-sized pieces

1 medium yellow onion, peeled and diced

8 ounces white mushrooms, sliced

$^1/_2$ teaspoon kosher salt

$^1/_4$ teaspoon ground black pepper

1 tablespoon Italian seasoning

1 (14-ounce) can artichoke hearts, drained and chopped

8 ounces fresh spinach, chopped

6 cloves garlic, peeled and minced

1 cup heavy cream

1 cup shredded Parmesan cheese

1. Preheat griddle to medium. Add oil and then chicken, onion, mushrooms, salt, pepper, and Italian seasoning. Cook 6 minutes, stirring with spatulas.

2. Add artichokes, spinach, and garlic. Cook 2 more minutes, stirring a few times.

3. Add cream and cheese. Mix it all together and cook 1–2 more minutes until cream thickens. Serve warm.

PER SERVING

Calories: **578**

Fat: **40g**

Protein: **41g**

Sodium: **771mg**

Fiber: **2g**

Carbohydrates: **10g**

Sugar: **4g**

Chicken Avocado Burgers

This is a unique and healthy burger option on the flat top. These burgers are delicate, so be gentle when flipping them. Serve with lettuce, tomato, spicy mayonnaise, and any other topping you like.

PREP TIME: 10 minutes   **COOK TIME: 12 minutes**   **SERVES: 4**

1 pound ground chicken

1 medium avocado, peeled, pitted, and diced

3 cloves garlic, peeled and finely minced

$1/2$ teaspoon kosher salt

$1/4$ teaspoon ground black pepper

2 tablespoons olive oil

4 brioche burger buns

1. Put chicken, avocado, garlic, salt, and pepper in a medium bowl. With your hands, combine, then divide and form 4 burger patties.
2. Preheat griddle to medium. Add oil and then burgers. Cook 5–6 minutes per side until browned and cooked through.
3. Place buns, cut sides down, on griddle and allow them to toast a few seconds to your desired darkness.
4. Serve burgers on buns.

PER SERVING
Calories: **433**
Fat: **21g**
Protein: **25g**

Sodium: **569mg**
Fiber: **3g**
Carbohydrates: **36g**
Sugar: **7g**

Street Corn Chicken Tacos

Street corn is typically a snack or side dish of corn on the cob slathered with a creamy sauce and rolled in cotija cheese. This recipe transforms it into a complete taco dinner on the Blackstone.

PREP TIME: 15 minutes   **COOK TIME: 12 minutes**   **SERVES: 4**

2 tablespoons vegetable oil, divided

1$\frac{1}{2}$ pounds boneless, skinless chicken thighs, cut into bite-sized pieces

4 ears corn, kernels cut off cobs

$\frac{3}{4}$ teaspoon kosher salt

$\frac{1}{4}$ teaspoon ground black pepper

1 (4-ounce) can diced green chiles

$\frac{3}{4}$ cup sour cream

$\frac{1}{2}$ cup mayonnaise

2 teaspoons chili powder

12 (5-inch) corn tortillas

$\frac{1}{2}$ cup chopped cilantro

$\frac{3}{4}$ cup crumbled cotija cheese

1. Preheat griddle to medium. Add 1 tablespoon oil, chicken, corn, salt, and pepper. Cook 8 minutes, stirring with spatulas a few times.
2. Add green chiles, sour cream, mayonnaise, and chili powder. Cook and stir 2 more minutes until combined. Remove and set aside. Clean Blackstone surface.
3. Add remaining 1 tablespoon oil and tortillas to griddle. Cook 1–2 minutes, flipping a few times, until as crisp as you prefer.
4. Serve tortillas with chicken and corn filling, topped with cilantro and cheese.

Tips for Cutting Corn

If you don't have a corn scraper, you can place a smaller bowl, upside down, inside of a larger bowl. Rest the corn cob on the smaller bowl and use a sharp knife to cut the kernels off. The smaller bowl provides a stable base, while the larger bowl catches the kernels for easy cleanup.

PER SERVING

Calories: **857**

Fat: **50g**

Protein: **41g**

Sodium: **1,170mg**

Fiber: **8g**

Carbohydrates: **56g**

Sugar: **9g**

Chicken Sausage with Sweet Potatoes and Apples

This dinner recipe gives off all the fall flavor vibes. It's on the healthier side and reheats very well, making it a great make-ahead meal.

PREP TIME: 15 minutes   **COOK TIME: 20 minutes**   **SERVES: 4**

2 tablespoons olive oil, divided

2 medium sweet potatoes (with skin), diced

1 cup chicken broth, divided

1 medium yellow onion, peeled and diced

1/2 teaspoon kosher salt

1/4 teaspoon ground black pepper

1 pound smoked chicken sausage, sliced

2 medium Honeycrisp apples (with peel), cored and diced

6 cups chopped spinach

2 teaspoons dried thyme

2 teaspoons paprika

1 teaspoon ground cumin

1/2 teaspoon ground cinnamon

1/4 cup pure maple syrup

1. Preheat griddle to medium. Add 1 tablespoon oil and then add sweet potatoes. Pour 2 tablespoons broth on sweet potatoes, then cover them with a melting dome or lid for 8 minutes. Remove dome a few times to flip potatoes, adding a little more broth each time. Be sure to reserve 1/3 cup broth.
2. Set melting dome aside. Add remaining 1 tablespoon oil, onion, salt, and pepper. Cook 4 minutes, using spatulas to combine everything.
3. Add sausage, apples, and spinach. Cook 6 minutes, mixing a few times with spatulas.
4. Add remaining 1/3 cup broth, thyme, paprika, cumin, cinnamon, and maple syrup. Cook and stir 1–2 more minutes until thickened, then serve.

PER SERVING

Calories: **405**

Fat: **16g**

Protein: **24g**

Sodium: **1,253mg**

Fiber: **6g**

Carbohydrates: **47g**

Sugar: **26g**

Gochujang Chicken Bites

These chicken bites can be served in wraps or tacos with their sauce and some added kimchi. Or you could prepare them ahead to eat over rice with the gochujang/mayonnaise sauce drizzled over the top. Feel free to use chicken breasts in place of the thighs if you prefer.

PREP TIME: 2 hours, 15 minutes*   **COOK TIME: 10 minutes**   **SERVES: 6**

3 tablespoons gochujang

3 tablespoons soy sauce

1 tablespoon lime juice

1 tablespoon honey

4 cloves garlic, peeled and minced

$1/2$ cup mayonnaise

$2^1/2$ pounds boneless, skinless chicken thighs, cut into bite-sized pieces

2 tablespoons vegetable oil

1 cup chopped cilantro

About Gochujang

Gochujang is a fermented red chili paste with a sweet and spicy flavor. It is very popular in Korean cooking and often used as a condiment. You can find gochujang in the Asian section of most large grocery stores, in Asian markets, or online.

1. To make marinade, put gochujang, soy sauce, lime juice, honey, and garlic in a small bowl. Stir until combined.

2. To make gochujang/mayonnaise sauce, in a separate small bowl, combine mayonnaise and 2 tablespoons of marinade. Cover and refrigerate until ready to use.

3. Put chicken in a sealable 1-gallon plastic bag with remaining marinade. Massage bag until chicken is coated. Marinate in refrigerator for 2–3 hours or overnight.

4. Preheat griddle to medium. Add oil and chicken. Cook 9–10 minutes, mixing with spatulas a few times, until chicken is cooked through. During last minute of cooking, add and mix in cilantro.

5. Serve with gochujang/mayonnaise sauce for dipping.

*Includes marinating time.

PER SERVING

Calories: **428**

Fat: **28g**

Protein: **34g**

Sodium: **652mg**

Fiber: **1g**

Carbohydrates: **5g**

Sugar: **4g**

Chicken Cordon Bleu

This is a very simple version of a classic dish. You could serve this chicken on a griddle-toasted burger bun to enjoy as a sandwich. For even more flavor, sprinkle the chicken with any seasoning blend that you like.

PREP TIME: 5 minutes   **COOK TIME: 8 minutes**   **SERVES: 4**

1/4 cup mayonnaise

2 tablespoons Dijon mustard

4 (4-ounce) thin-cut chicken breasts

1/2 teaspoon kosher salt

1/4 teaspoon ground black pepper

1 tablespoon olive oil

1/2 pound sliced deli ham

8 (1-ounce) slices Swiss cheese

1. To make sauce, put mayonnaise and mustard in a small bowl; stir until combined.
2. Season chicken on both sides with salt and pepper.
3. Preheat griddle to medium. Add oil and then chicken. Cook 4 minutes and then flip chicken.
4. After flipping chicken, put the slices of ham on the Blackstone for 1 minute. Spread prepared sauce over each chicken breast. Top each chicken breast with ham and cheese.
5. Cook 4 more minutes, covering with a melting dome or lid during the last few minutes of cooking time. Serve once cheese is melted.

PER SERVING

Calories: **530**

Fat: **32g**

Protein: **50g**

Sodium: **1,117mg**

Fiber: **0g**

Carbohydrates: **5g**

Sugar: **2g**

Pineapple Chicken Stir-Fry

This dish will transport you to the warm tropics with its Caribbean flavors, bright colors, and fresh ingredients. If you like, serve with a store-bought Caribbean jerk sauce on the side.

PREP TIME: 25 minutes   **COOK TIME: 10 minutes**   **SERVES: 6**

2 tablespoons olive oil

2 pounds boneless, skinless chicken thighs, cut into bite-sized pieces

1 medium red onion, peeled and sliced

1 medium red bell pepper, seeded and sliced

1 medium orange bell pepper, seeded and sliced

3 medium jalapeño peppers, seeded and sliced

2 tablespoons Caribbean jerk seasoning

$1/2$ teaspoon kosher salt

$1/4$ teaspoon ground black pepper

6 cloves garlic, peeled and minced

2 tablespoons soy sauce

1 medium pineapple, peeled, cored, and diced

1 cup chopped cilantro

2 tablespoons lime juice

1. Preheat griddle to medium. Add oil, chicken, onion, bell peppers, jalapeños, jerk seasoning, salt, and black pepper. Cook 6 minutes, stirring with spatulas a few times.

2. Add garlic, soy sauce, and pineapple. Cook 3 more minutes, mixing everything together.

3. Add cilantro and lime juice, cook and stir 1 more minute, and then serve.

PER SERVING
Calories: **326**
Fat: **11g**
Protein: **28g**
Sodium: **715mg**
Fiber: **4g**
Carbohydrates: **27g**
Sugar: **18g**

Lemon Feta Chicken Kebabs

These kebabs are wonderful served with the homemade naan in Chapter 4. It's a healthy and fresh dinner recipe with bright flavors.

PREP TIME: 2 hours, 25 minutes*   **COOK TIME: 12 minutes**   **SERVES: 6**

2 (5.3-ounce) containers nonfat plain Greek yogurt

2 tablespoons mayonnaise

2 tablespoons lemon juice

2 ounces crumbled feta cheese

2 teaspoons dried oregano

2 pounds boneless, skinless chicken breasts, cut into 1-inch pieces

1/2 teaspoon kosher salt

1/4 teaspoon ground black pepper

2 medium red bell peppers, seeded and cut into 1-inch pieces

1 large red onion, peeled and cut into 1-inch pieces

2 tablespoons olive oil

1. To prepare yogurt sauce, in a medium bowl, stir yogurt, mayonnaise, lemon juice, cheese, and oregano until combined.

2. Put chicken in a sealable 1-gallon plastic bag with 1/3 cup prepared yogurt sauce, salt, and black pepper. Massage bag until chicken is coated and marinate in the refrigerator for 2–3 hours or overnight. Cover and refrigerate remaining sauce until ready to use.

3. Assemble kebabs using 6 wooden or metal skewers, alternating chicken, bell peppers, and onion.

4. Preheat griddle to medium. Add oil and then kebabs. Cook 10–12 minutes, turning several times. Remove once chicken is cooked through and vegetables are tender with a slight char.

5. Serve kebabs with remaining yogurt sauce on the side.

*Includes marinating time.

PER SERVING

Calories: **266**

Fat: **10g**

Protein: **38g**

Sodium: **276mg**

Fiber: **1g**

Carbohydrates: **7g**

Sugar: **4g**

Chicken Corn Zucchini Stir-Fry

There is a gorgeous mix of colors in this light and healthy Blackstone dinner. You can also try adding a seasoning blend or some fresh or dried herbs to create your own unique flavor profile.

PREP TIME: 15 minutes   **COOK TIME: 11 minutes**   **SERVES: 4**

2 tablespoons olive oil

4 ears corn, kernels cut off cobs

2 medium zucchini, cut into 1-inch pieces (about 3 cups)

1 pint grape tomatoes (whole)

1 pound boneless, skinless chicken thighs, cut into bite-sized pieces

1/2 teaspoon kosher salt

1/4 teaspoon ground black pepper

6 cloves garlic, peeled and minced

2 tablespoons lemon juice

1. Preheat griddle to medium. Add oil and then corn; cook 2 minutes, tossing with spatulas.

2. Add zucchini, tomatoes, chicken, salt, pepper, and garlic. Cook 8–9 more minutes or until vegetables are tender. Mix in lemon juice during the last minute of cooking time. Serve.

PER SERVING
Calories: **306**
Fat: **12g**
Protein: **24g**
Sodium: **347mg**
Fiber: **4g**
Carbohydrates: **27g**
Sugar: **11g**

Barbecue Chicken Garlic Toast Pizzas

Here is a quick and easy dinner that's sure to make everyone do the happy dinner dance. You can add some variety to these garlic toast pizzas by using pesto in place of the barbecue sauce, or you could make a simple pepperoni-and-pizza-sauce version.

PREP TIME: **5 minutes**   COOK TIME: **5 minutes**   SERVES: **4**

1^1/2 cups cooked, chopped chicken

1 teaspoon barbecue seasoning

1 (14-ounce, 8-count) thawed package frozen garlic toast

1 cup barbecue sauce

2 cups shredded mozzarella cheese

Meal Prep Chicken

About once a week, try cooking a few thin-cut chicken breasts on your griddle to use for meals over the next several days. Sprinkle with any seasoning blend you prefer, add olive oil to your Blackstone over medium heat, and cook chicken 7–8 minutes, flipping it a few times. Cut, cover, and store in the refrigerator to use in pizzas, salads, or wraps, or as a snack.

1. In a medium bowl, toss chicken and barbecue seasoning together.
2. Preheat griddle to medium-low. Place garlic toast on Blackstone, cook 2 minutes, and then flip.
3. Top each piece with barbecue sauce, chicken, and cheese. Cover with a melting dome or lid 2–3 minutes or until cheese is melted, then serve.

PER SERVING

Calories: **740**

Fat: **32g**

Protein: **34g**

Sodium: **1,822mg**

Fiber: **1g**

Carbohydrates: **75g**

Sugar: **25g**

Italian Chicken Kebabs

These kebabs can be made in advance and stored in the refrigerator on a tray until ready to cook. Or skip the skewers altogether and make this dish into a yummy stir-fry.

PREP TIME: 2 hours, 25 minutes*   **COOK TIME: 12 minutes**   **SERVES: 6**

1^1/2 pounds boneless, skinless chicken breasts, cut into 1-inch pieces

^{3}/4 cup Italian dressing, divided

4 cloves garlic, peeled and minced

1 tablespoon Italian seasoning

^{3}/4 teaspoon kosher salt

^{1}/2 teaspoon ground black pepper

1 medium red onion, peeled and cut into 1-inch pieces

1 medium red bell pepper, seeded and cut into 1-inch pieces

1 medium zucchini, cut into 1-inch pieces

1 medium yellow squash, cut into 1-inch pieces

2 tablespoons olive oil

1. To a sealable 1-gallon plastic bag, add chicken, half of Italian dressing, garlic, Italian seasoning, salt, and black pepper. Massage bag until combined, and marinate in the refrigerator for 2–3 hours or overnight.
2. Assemble kebabs on wooden or metal skewers, alternating chicken, onion, bell pepper, zucchini, and squash.
3. Preheat griddle to medium. Add oil and then kebabs.
4. Cook 10–12 minutes, turning several times. During the last 4 minutes of cooking time, brush with remaining Italian dressing. Remove once chicken and vegetables are cooked through and charred to your preference. Serve.

*Includes marinating time.

PER SERVING

Calories: **218**
Fat: **9g**
Protein: **27g**
Sodium: **443mg**
Fiber: **1g**
Carbohydrates: **7g**
Sugar: **5g**

Pesto Chicken Pizza

You have many dough options when making pizza at home. You can make your own or buy pizza dough from a grocery store or local pizza restaurant. You can also use precooked pizza crust or flatbread. If using a precooked crust, take a few minutes off the cook time of this recipe.

PREP TIME: 10 minutes   **COOK TIME: 12 minutes**   **SERVES: 4**

1 pound pizza dough

1 tablespoon olive oil

1 cup pesto

1 cup cooked, chopped chicken

2 cups shredded mozzarella cheese

4 ounces sliced sun-dried tomatoes

1. Roll pizza dough into a circle approximately 16 inches in diameter.
2. Preheat griddle to medium-low. Add oil and place pizza dough on griddle. Cook 3–4 minutes and then flip.
3. Spread pesto evenly on crust; add chicken, cheese, and sun-dried tomatoes. Cover with melting dome or lid for 4–8 minutes until cheese is melted and crust is cooked through. Cook time will depend on thickness of dough. Slice and serve.

PER SERVING

Calories: **772**

Fat: **35g**

Protein: **37g**

Sodium: **1,652mg**

Fiber: **6g**

Carbohydrates: **78g**

Sugar: **19g**

Chicken Caesar Tortellini Salads

The tortellini in this recipe become crisp on the outside and soft on the inside—the perfect addition to a cool, crunchy salad. Make this dinner even easier by simply combining your griddle-cooked tortellini with a store-bought Caesar salad kit.

PREP TIME: 10 minutes   **COOK TIME: 9 minutes**   **SERVES: 4**

1 (10-ounce) bag frozen cheese tortellini, thawed

1 tablespoon olive oil

1 pound boneless, skinless chicken breasts, cut into bite-sized pieces

1/2 teaspoon kosher salt

1/4 teaspoon ground black pepper

3 cloves garlic, peeled and minced

3 romaine hearts, chopped

1/3 cup shredded Parmesan cheese

6 ounces Caesar salad dressing

1. Preheat griddle to medium. Place tortellini on one side of the Blackstone, add 2 tablespoons water, and then cover with a melting dome or lid. Add oil, chicken, salt, and pepper to other side of griddle. Cook everything 5 minutes, stirring a few times and adding 2 more tablespoons water to tortellini after mixing, before covering again.

2. After 5 minutes, remove dome, mix tortellini and chicken together, add garlic, and cook 3–4 more minutes until chicken is cooked through.

3. Let cool slightly. Place lettuce in a large bowl with cheese, Caesar dressing, chicken, and tortellini. Toss together before serving.

PER SERVING
Calories: **556**
Fat: **26g**
Protein: **42g**
Sodium: **922mg**
Fiber: **14g**
Carbohydrates: **43g**
Sugar: **6g**

Smashed Chicken Gyro Tacos

The homemade yogurt sauce in this recipe is so good, it's a keeper all by itself. You could also use ground lamb in place of the chicken for a more authentic gyro experience.

PREP TIME: 15 minutes   **COOK TIME: 6 minutes**   **SERVES: 4**

1 (5.3-ounce) container nonfat plain Greek yogurt

3 tablespoons mayonnaise

1 medium cucumber, shredded

1 tablespoon lemon juice

1 pound ground chicken

4 cloves garlic, peeled and finely minced

1 tablespoon dried oregano

1/2 tablespoon paprika

1/2 teaspoon kosher salt

1/4 teaspoon ground black pepper

1 tablespoon olive oil

8 (6-inch) flour tortillas

1 1/2 cups shredded lettuce

4 ounces crumbled feta cheese

1. In a small bowl, stir yogurt, mayonnaise, cucumber, and lemon juice until combined.

2. In a medium bowl, using your hands, combine chicken, garlic, oregano, paprika, salt, and pepper. Divide evenly and roll into 8 balls.

3. Preheat griddle to medium. Add oil and place balls of chicken on the Blackstone, leaving 6 inches between them. Cover each with a tortilla. Use a burger press to smash each one to flatten.

4. Cook 4 minutes, flip, and cook another 1–2 minutes until tortilla is crisped to your liking. Serve topped with yogurt sauce, lettuce, and cheese, and folded in half like a taco.

PER SERVING

Calories: **531**

Fat: **27g**

Protein: **32g**

Sodium: **1,066mg**

Fiber: **3g**

Carbohydrates: **39g**

Sugar: **6g**

Southwest Chicken, Corn, and Beans

This healthy dish is great to make ahead. To indulge a bit, you could top yours with cheese and sour cream and add some crushed tortilla chips for texture.

PREP TIME: **10 minutes**   COOK TIME: **10 minutes**   SERVES: **6**

2 tablespoons vegetable oil

1$^{1}/_{2}$ pounds boneless, skinless chicken thighs, cut into bite-sized pieces

1 medium yellow onion, peeled and diced

$^{1}/_{2}$ teaspoon kosher salt

$^{1}/_{4}$ teaspoon ground black pepper

2 tablespoons taco seasoning

5 cloves garlic, peeled and minced

1 (14-ounce) can corn, drained

1 (14-ounce) can black beans, drained and rinsed

1 (14-ounce) jar salsa

1. Preheat griddle to medium. Add oil, chicken, onion, salt, and pepper. Cook 6 minutes, tossing with spatulas.
2. Add taco seasoning, garlic, corn, beans, and salsa. Cook 4 more minutes, mixing everything together, and then serve.

PER SERVING

Calories: **291**

Fat: **9g**

Protein: **24g**

Sodium: **1,145mg**

Fiber: **8g**

Carbohydrates: **25g**

Sugar: **6g**

Beef and Pork Main Dishes

While lots of people love a steak and potatoes dinner, sometimes it's nice to think outside the box. In this chapter you'll find incredible recipes for steak, sausage, ham, and pork. Packing tons of protein, along with iron, zinc, and B vitamins, beef and pork are foods you don't want to skip over. And with the Blackstone griddle you don't have to, because you can cook up these delicious meats quickly, easily, and with little mess.

In this chapter you will find dishes like Flank Steak Caprese, Sausage Sweet Potato Hash, Steak and Mushroom Burritos, Gochujang Pork Rice Bowls, and The Ultimate Smash Burgers—a Blackstone griddle sensation! You'll also discover more sophisticated dishes like Garlic Herb Pork Tenderloin and Apple Bourbon Pork Chops. Whether you're craving classic dishes to cook on your griddle or looking for some new favorites, this chapter has you covered!

Steak and Pierogi

Pierogi are soft, pillowy dumplings filled with cheese, onions, or (in this case) potatoes. This spin on the classic combo of steak and potatoes includes a cheesy, creamy sauce that will have you coming back for seconds.

PREP TIME: 15 minutes   **COOK TIME: 13 minutes**   **SERVES: 6**

1 (16-ounce) package frozen cheddar and potato pierogi, thawed

2 tablespoons olive oil

1 medium yellow onion, peeled and diced

8 ounces white mushrooms, sliced

2 pounds sirloin steak, cut into bite-sized pieces

1/2 teaspoon kosher salt

1/4 teaspoon ground black pepper

2 teaspoons steak seasoning

8 ounces spinach, chopped

6 cloves garlic, peeled and minced

1 cup heavy cream

1/2 cup shredded Parmesan cheese

1. Preheat griddle to medium. Add pierogi, squirt them with 2 tablespoons water, and cover with a melting dome or lid for 3 minutes. Halfway through the cooking time, flip pierogi with tongs and add 2 more tablespoons water before covering again.

2. Remove melting dome and add oil, onion, and mushrooms. Cook 4 minutes, stirring with spatulas.

3. Add steak, salt, pepper, steak seasoning, spinach, and garlic. Toss and cook 4 more minutes.

4. Pour cream onto mixture and sprinkle with cheese. Cook 1–2 more minutes until cream thickens into a sauce and then serve.

PER SERVING
Calories: **631**
Fat: **36g**
Protein: **42g**

Sodium: **943mg**
Fiber: **2g**
Carbohydrates: **28g**
Sugar: **3g**

Italian Sausage Sloppy Joes

This dish is an open-faced version of the classic sloppy joe sandwich. This take is served on garlic toast, but you can swap in traditional burger buns if you prefer.

PREP TIME: 5 minutes   **COOK TIME: 13 minutes**   **SERVES: 4**

1 tablespoon olive oil

1 medium yellow onion, peeled and diced

1 pound ground Italian sausage

2 teaspoons Italian seasoning

$1/4$ teaspoon kosher salt

$2^{1}/2$ cups marinara sauce

8 slices frozen garlic toast, thawed

8 (1-ounce) slices provolone cheese

4 basil leaves, sliced

1. Preheat griddle to medium. Add oil, onion, sausage, Italian seasoning, and salt. Cook 8 minutes, breaking sausage apart with spatulas.

2. Add marinara sauce to sausage and mix with spatulas for 1 minute. Scoot this mixture to edge of griddle and scrape center of griddle clean.

3. Place garlic toast in center of Blackstone for about 2 minutes per side or until toasted and golden brown. Place a slice of cheese on each toast and then top with sausage mixture.

4. Garnish with basil and serve.

PER SERVING

Calories: **951**

Fat: **67g**

Protein: **34g**

Sodium: **2,835mg**

Fiber: **4g**

Carbohydrates: **51g**

Sugar: **11g**

Balsamic Sausage and Peppers

This recipe is fabulous as is, but there are a few ways you could amp it up. You could top it with crumbled goat cheese or feta and fresh basil. You could also serve it on griddle-toasted sub buns for a unique sausage and pepper sandwich.

PREP TIME: 15 minutes   **COOK TIME: 10 minutes**   **SERVES: 4**

2 tablespoons olive oil

1 medium red bell pepper, seeded and sliced

1 medium yellow bell pepper, seeded and sliced

1 medium yellow onion, peeled and sliced

1 teaspoon dried oregano

1/2 teaspoon kosher salt

1/4 teaspoon ground black pepper

1 pound smoked sausage, sliced

6 cloves garlic, peeled and minced

2 tablespoons balsamic vinegar

2 ounces balsamic glaze

1. Preheat griddle to medium. Add oil, bell peppers, onion, oregano, salt, and black pepper. Cook 5 minutes, stirring with spatulas.
2. Add sausage, garlic, and vinegar. Cook 5 more minutes, tossing a few times.
3. Drizzle balsamic glaze over top and serve.

Balsamic Glaze

Balsamic glaze has a slightly sweet and tangy flavor. You can find it in the vinegar section of most large grocery stores or order it online. It usually comes in a squeeze bottle, so it's easy to drizzle.

PER SERVING
Calories: **408**
Fat: **27g**
Protein: **12g**

Sodium: **1,015mg**
Fiber: **2g**
Carbohydrates: **24g**
Sugar: **18g**

Crispy Breaded Pork Chops

This simple dinner is ready in just a few minutes. You can mix it up with different seasoning blends or dipping sauces of choice. These chops are also incredible served as sandwiches with toppings of your choice.

PREP TIME: 10 minutes   **COOK TIME: 8 minutes**   **SERVES: 4**

1 large egg

1 cup panko bread crumbs

1/2 teaspoon kosher salt

1/4 teaspoon ground black pepper

4 (4-ounce) boneless pork chops

2 tablespoons olive oil

1. Crack egg into a medium bowl and beat with a fork. In a separate medium bowl, stir panko, salt, and pepper until combined.
2. Dip each pork chop into egg, coating both sides, then panko mixture. Press panko into the pork so it sticks.
3. Preheat griddle to medium. Add oil and pork chops. Cook 3–4 minutes per side until breading is crisp and golden brown. Serve warm.

PER SERVING

Calories: **289**

Fat: **11g**

Protein: **27g**

Sodium: **350mg**

Fiber: **0g**

Carbohydrates: **16g**

Sugar: **1g**

Skirt Steak with Corn Relish

Skirt steak is a very thin cut of meat, so it has an extra-quick cooking time. Slice against the grain for maximum tenderness. Skirt steaks usually come pre-seasoned; if yours does not, season it with kosher salt and pepper before cooking.

PREP TIME: 15 minutes   **COOK TIME: 11 minutes**   **SERVES: 6**

1 (2-pound) skirt steak

$4^1/2$ teaspoons taco seasoning, divided

$3/4$ teaspoon kosher salt, divided

$1/2$ teaspoon ground black pepper, divided

2 tablespoons vegetable oil, divided

4 ears corn, kernels cut off cobs

1 small red onion, peeled and diced

3 medium jalapeño peppers, seeded and diced

6 cloves garlic, peeled and minced

$1/2$ cup chopped cilantro

2 tablespoons lime juice

Making Steak Tacos

Another way to enjoy this recipe is as a filling for tacos. You could warm flour or corn tortillas on the griddle or warm mini naan for a unique taco experience. Add steak, relish, and other toppings of choice, such as cheese, sour cream, and hot sauce.

1. Season both sides of steak using $2^1/4$ teaspoons taco seasoning, $1/2$ teaspoon salt, and $1/4$ teaspoon pepper.

2. Preheat griddle to medium. Add 1 tablespoon oil, corn, onion, jalapeños, and remaining $2^1/4$ teaspoons taco seasoning, $1/4$ teaspoon salt, and $1/4$ teaspoon pepper. Cook 4 minutes, tossing with spatulas.

3. Add garlic to corn mixture. Add remaining 1 tablespoon oil to empty side of griddle, then add steak and cook 2–3 minutes per side until your desired doneness. Meanwhile, continue mixing corn with spatulas a few times.

4. Remove steak from griddle and allow to rest. Add cilantro and lime juice to corn mixture, mix, and cook 1 more minute.

5. Slice steak and serve with corn relish on top.

PER SERVING

Calories: **310**

Fat: **13g**

Protein: **30g**

Sodium: **484mg**

Fiber: **2g**

Carbohydrates: **17g**

Sugar: **5g**

Carne Asada Tacos

Carne asada is a traditional Mexican dish of grilled and sliced marinated steak. This version wraps bite-sized steak pieces in corn tortillas. Substitute pickled red onions for the diced onions if you like.

PREP TIME: 2 hours, 20 minutes*   **COOK TIME: 10 minutes**   **SERVES: 4**

1 large bunch cilantro, divided

$1/4$ cup lime juice

$1/4$ cup orange juice

4 tablespoons vegetable oil, divided

3 cloves garlic, peeled

2 teaspoons honey

2 teaspoons chili powder

2 teaspoons paprika

1 teaspoon ground cumin

$1/4$ teaspoon ground cinnamon

$1/2$ teaspoon kosher salt

$1/4$ teaspoon ground black pepper

$1^1/2$ pounds flat iron steak (cut into bite-sized pieces)

12 (5-inch) corn tortillas

$1/2$ cup crumbled cotija cheese

$1/2$ cup diced white onion

1. To make sauce, in a food processor or blender, blend half of cilantro, lime juice, orange juice, 2 tablespoons oil, garlic, honey, chili powder, paprika, cumin, cinnamon, salt, and pepper until smooth, about 1 minute.

2. Put steak in a sealable 1-gallon plastic bag. Add half of prepared sauce and massage bag until combined. Allow to marinate in the refrigerator for 2–3 hours or overnight. Cover remaining sauce and store in refrigerator.

3. Preheat griddle to medium. Add 1 tablespoon oil and then steak. Cook 6 minutes, tossing with spatulas. Remove, set aside, and scrape griddle.

4. Add remaining 1 tablespoon oil and tortillas to griddle. Cook 1–2 minutes per side until as crisp as you like.

5. Chop remaining cilantro. Serve steak in tortillas, topped with remaining sauce, cheese, chopped cilantro, and onions.

*Includes marinating time.

PER SERVING

Calories: **584**
Fat: **26g**
Protein: **45g**
Sodium: **520mg**
Fiber: **6g**
Carbohydrates: **42g**
Sugar: **6g**

Flank Steak Caprese

This steak dinner looks beautiful, and it tastes just as amazing. The cook time on the steak is for medium rare; add another minute per side for medium.

PREP TIME: 10 minutes   **COOK TIME: 8 minutes**   **SERVES: 4**

1 (1½-pound) flank steak

½ teaspoon kosher salt

¼ teaspoon ground black pepper

2 tablespoons olive oil

1 tablespoon balsamic vinegar

1 pint cherry tomatoes (whole)

2 ounces balsamic glaze

4 ounces fresh mozzarella cheese, cut into bite-sized pieces

8 basil leaves, sliced

1. Season steak on both sides with salt and pepper.
2. Preheat griddle to medium. Add oil, then put steak on one side of the Blackstone and tomatoes on the other side. Cook steak 3 minutes per side; meanwhile, use spatulas to toss tomatoes a few times.
3. Remove steak and set aside. Add vinegar to tomatoes and cook 2 more minutes, stirring occasionally.
4. Slice steak against the grain and top with tomatoes, balsamic glaze, cheese, and basil. Serve.

PER SERVING

Calories: **469**

Fat: **21g**

Protein: **45g**

Sodium: **509mg**

Fiber: **1g**

Carbohydrates: **19g**

Sugar: **16g**

Reuben in a Bowl

This recipe is a lower-carb version of the classic Reuben sandwich. This recipe works well to prepare ahead if you divide it into containers with the dressing on the side. It can stay fresh in the refrigerator for a few days. Reheat it in the microwave for a tasty meal on the go.

PREP TIME: 10 minutes   **COOK TIME: 10 minutes**   **SERVES: 4**

1 tablespoon olive oil

1 medium yellow onion, peeled and diced

1/4 teaspoon kosher salt

1 (24-ounce) bag coleslaw mix

3 tablespoons Worcestershire sauce

1 pound deli pastrami, diced

2 cups sauerkraut

12 (1-ounce) slices Swiss cheese, diced

4 medium scallions, sliced

1/2 cup Russian dressing

1. Preheat griddle to medium. Add oil, onion, and salt and cook 3 minutes, stirring with spatulas.
2. Add coleslaw and Worcestershire sauce and cook 5 minutes, tossing a few times.
3. Add pastrami, sauerkraut, cheese, and scallions. Cook 2 more minutes. Serve in bowls with Russian dressing drizzled on top.

PER SERVING
Calories: **792**
Fat: **38g**
Protein: **54g**
Sodium: **1,646mg**
Fiber: **13g**
Carbohydrates: **55g**
Sugar: **28g**

Cheesesteak Tortellini

This cheesesteak may not be from Philly, but it's a creamy, cheesy pasta dish on the Blackstone that's out-of-this-world delicious! Feel free to leave out the bell peppers and onions if they are not to your liking.

PREP TIME: 15 minutes   **COOK TIME: 13 minutes**   **SERVES: 6**

1 (20-ounce) bag frozen cheese tortellini, thawed

2 tablespoons olive oil

1 medium yellow onion, peeled and sliced

1 medium green bell pepper, seeded and sliced

8 ounces white mushrooms, sliced

1$^1/_2$ pounds sirloin steak, cut into bite-sized pieces

6 cloves garlic, peeled and minced

2 teaspoons steak seasoning

$^3/_4$ teaspoon kosher salt

1$^1/_2$ cups heavy cream

1$^1/_2$ cups shredded mozzarella cheese

1. Preheat griddle to medium. Add tortellini, squirt 2 tablespoons water on top, and cover with a melting dome or lid for 3 minutes. Mix halfway through the cooking time, adding 2 more tablespoons water before covering again.

2. Remove dome and add oil, onion, pepper, and mushrooms. Cook 4 minutes, stirring with spatulas.

3. Add steak, garlic, steak seasoning, and salt. Cook 4 minutes, stirring and tossing.

4. Slowly pour cream and cheese on top and mix with spatulas until sauce thickens, about 1–2 minutes. Serve.

PER SERVING

Calories: **741**

Fat: **43g**

Protein: **42g**

Sodium: **981mg**

Fiber: **7g**

Carbohydrates: **42g**

Sugar: **5g**

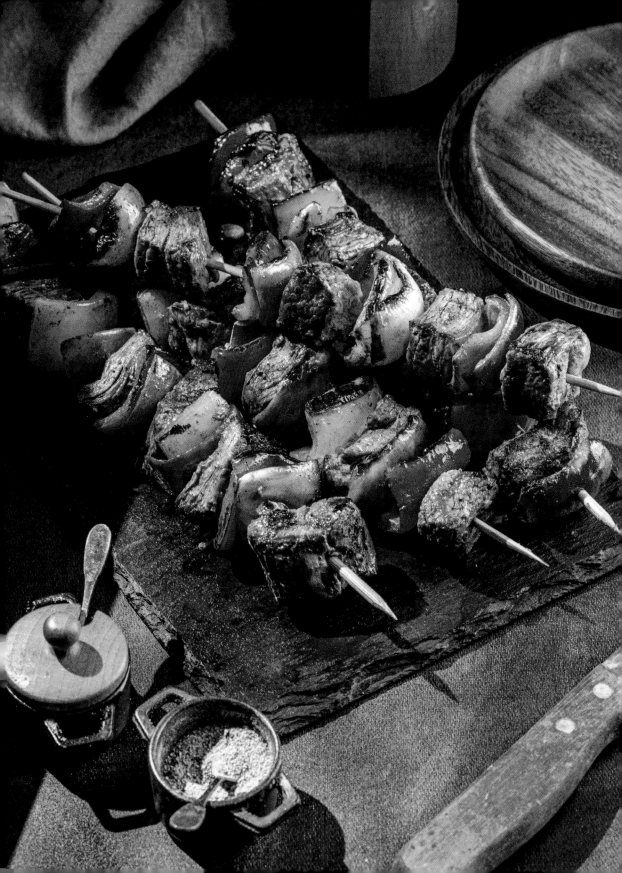

Steak Fajita Kebabs

This recipe is a low-carb way to enjoy fajitas. Another option is to skip the skewers, add the steak and vegetables to the griddle, and cook for the same amount of time, stirring with spatulas. You could serve the steak and vegetables with tortillas, topped with lettuce, cheese, and sour cream if desired.

PREP TIME: 35 minutes*   **COOK TIME: 10 minutes**   **SERVES: 4**

2 pounds flat iron steak, cut into 1-inch cubes

1 large yellow onion, peeled and cut into 1-inch pieces

1 large red bell pepper, seeded and cut into 1-inch pieces

1 large yellow bell pepper, seeded and cut into 1-inch pieces

3 tablespoons olive oil, divided

2 tablespoons soy sauce

2 tablespoons lime juice

2 tablespoons fajita seasoning

1/2 teaspoon kosher salt

4 cloves garlic, peeled and minced

Assembling the Kebabs

When cutting the steak and vegetables, aim for the same size. Each piece will cook more evenly and will touch the Blackstone surface to get a nice sear on all sides. These kebabs can be assembled several hours before cooking.

1. Place steak cubes in a medium bowl. Place onion and peppers in another medium bowl.
2. In a small bowl, whisk 2 tablespoons oil, soy sauce, lime juice, fajita seasoning, salt, and garlic until combined. Add 1 tablespoon of this sauce to vegetables and remainder to steak, toss both until evenly coated, and marinate 15 minutes on the countertop.
3. Arrange steak and vegetables on 8 kebab skewers, alternating steak and vegetables on each skewer. (If using wooden skewers, there's no need to soak them, as the flat top does not have an open flame.)
4. Preheat griddle to medium. Add remaining 1 tablespoon oil to griddle and then place kebabs on griddle. Cook 8–10 minutes, flipping a few times, until vegetables are tender. Serve.

*Includes marinating time.

PER SERVING
Calories: **476**
Fat: **26g**
Protein: **49g**
Sodium: **579mg**
Fiber: **2g**
Carbohydrates: **11g**
Sugar: **3g**

Sausage Sweet Potato Hash

This complete meal on the Blackstone seems like the perfect fall dinner. Hash is typically made with white potatoes, but this recipe uses sweet potatoes for more nutrients and a sweeter, richer taste. This dish is a great one to prepare ahead.

PREP TIME: 10 minutes　　**COOK TIME: 18 minutes**　　**SERVES: 4**

2 tablespoons olive oil, divided

2 medium sweet potatoes (with skin), diced

1/2 teaspoon kosher salt

1/4 teaspoon ground black pepper

1 pound ground pork sausage

2 medium Honeycrisp apples (with peel), cored and diced

1 teaspoon paprika

1 teaspoon dried thyme

1/2 teaspoon ground cumin

1/4 teaspoon ground cinnamon

1. Preheat griddle to medium. Add 1 tablespoon oil and sweet potatoes. Squirt 3 tablespoons water over the potatoes and cover with melting dome or lid for 9 minutes. Remove dome to flip them a few times, each time adding 3 more tablespoons water before covering again.

2. Set dome aside and add remaining 1 tablespoon oil, salt, pepper, sausage, and apples. Cook 8 minutes, mixing with spatulas a few times.

3. Add paprika, thyme, cumin, cinnamon, and another squirt of water. Cook 1 more minute, mixing. Serve right away.

PER SERVING

Calories: **415**

Fat: **22g**

Protein: **26g**

Sodium: **357mg**

Fiber: **4g**

Carbohydrates: **26g**

Sugar: **12g**

Apple Bourbon Pork Chops

Pork and apples are a classic combination. The bourbon in this recipe adds flavor and fun, but you can omit it if desired. Decrease the cook time on the pork slightly if you are using boneless pork chops.

PREP TIME: 10 minutes   **COOK TIME: 8 minutes**   **SERVES: 4**

4 (6-ounce, 1-inch thick) bone-in pork chops

$1/2$ teaspoon kosher salt

$1/4$ teaspoon ground black pepper

2 medium Honeycrisp apples (with peel), cored and diced

1 tablespoon olive oil

4 tablespoons unsalted butter

2 tablespoons bourbon

2 tablespoons light brown sugar

$1/4$ teaspoon ground cinnamon

Brining the Pork

For extra-juicy and moist pork, follow these directions to brine: Add $1^1/2$ cups water, $1^1/2$ cups apple juice, $1/2$ cup light brown sugar, and $1/4$ cup kosher salt to a medium saucepan. Bring just to a boil and let cool. Pour brine over pork chops in a container and refrigerate 24 hours. Pat pork dry and discard brine. No need to season pork chops with more salt.

1. Season pork with salt and pepper on both sides.
2. Preheat griddle to medium. Put apples on one side of the Blackstone and add oil and pork on other side.
3. Cook everything 8 minutes total, flipping pork a few times and tossing apples with spatulas. During last 2 minutes of cooking time, add butter, bourbon, brown sugar, and cinnamon to apples, stirring to combine.
4. Serve pork topped with bourbon apples.

PER SERVING

Calories: **418**
Fat: **22g**
Protein: **36g**
Sodium: **351mg**
Fiber: **2g**
Carbohydrates: **19g**
Sugar: **16g**

Bacon Mushroom Melts

A cheesy sandwich on the Blackstone is a great comfort food. Add a side salad or bowl of soup and you have a complete and delicious meal.

PREP TIME: **10 minutes**   COOK TIME: **14 minutes**   SERVES: **4**

6 slices bacon, cut into bite-sized pieces

8 ounces white mushrooms, sliced

¼ teaspoon kosher salt

⅛ teaspoon ground black pepper

8 (1-ounce) slices marble rye bread

8 (1-ounce) slices Swiss cheese

2 tablespoons unsalted butter

1. Preheat griddle to medium. Add bacon, mushrooms, salt, and pepper. Cook 8 minutes, stirring with spatulas a few times. Remove and set aside. Scrape griddle and lower heat to medium-low.

2. To assemble sandwiches, lay 4 slices bread on a work surface. Add a slice of cheese to each, followed by a quarter of the mushroom bacon mixture, another slice of cheese, and a top slice of bread.

3. Add butter to the Blackstone and, once melted, place sandwiches on griddle. Cook about 2–3 minutes per side, flipping halfway through the cooking time until bread is toasty and cheese is melted. Serve right away.

PER SERVING

Calories: **492**

Fat: **26g**

Protein: **28g**

Sodium: **794mg**

Fiber: **4g**

Carbohydrates: **33g**

Sugar: **4g**

Ham, Potatoes, and Green Beans

Here is a classic comfort dish that's easily cooked on the Blackstone. Feel free to replace the Cajun seasoning with any seasoning blend that you love.

PREP TIME: 15 minutes   **COOK TIME: 18 minutes**   **SERVES: 4**

2 tablespoons olive oil, divided

1 pound red potatoes, diced

1 pound green beans, trimmed and cut into 2-inch pieces

1 medium yellow onion, peeled and diced

2 teaspoons Cajun seasoning

$1/2$ teaspoon kosher salt

$1/4$ teaspoon ground black pepper

1 pound ham steak, cut into 1-inch cubes

6 cloves garlic, peeled and minced

4 tablespoons unsalted butter

2 tablespoons lemon juice

1. Preheat griddle to medium. Add 1 tablespoon oil and potatoes. Squirt 3 tablespoons water over potatoes and cover with melting dome or lid for 5 minutes. Remove dome to stir a few times, adding 3 more tablespoons of water each time before covering again.
2. Set dome aside and add remaining 1 tablespoon oil, green beans, onion, Cajun seasoning, salt, and pepper. Cook 8 minutes, tossing a few times with spatulas.
3. Add ham, garlic, and butter. Cook 4 more minutes, stirring. Add lemon juice and mix 1 more minute before serving.

PER SERVING

Calories: **432**

Fat: **18g**

Protein: **32g**

Sodium: **459mg**

Fiber: **5g**

Carbohydrates: **34g**

Sugar: **6g**

Cowboy Stir-Fry with Sausage

They say cowboys love simple, hearty, budget-friendly meals like this recipe. You can top this dish with hot sauce and sour cream to add to the Tex-Mex theme if you like.

PREP TIME: **10 minutes**   COOK TIME: **13 minutes**   SERVES: **6**

5 slices bacon, cut into bite-sized pieces

1 (28-ounce) bag frozen potatoes with peppers and onions (potatoes O'Brien), thawed

3 cups chopped green cabbage

1 medium red bell pepper, seeded and sliced

2 medium jalapeño peppers, sliced, some seeds removed

1 pound smoked sausage, sliced

2 teaspoons chili powder

$1/2$ teaspoon kosher salt

$1/4$ teaspoon ground black pepper

$1/2$ teaspoon paprika

$1/2$ teaspoon garlic powder

2 tablespoons lime juice

1. Preheat griddle to medium. Add bacon, potatoes, cabbage, bell pepper, and jalapeños. Cook 4 minutes, mixing with spatulas.
2. Add sausage, chili powder, salt, black pepper, paprika, and garlic powder. Cook 8 more minutes, mixing. Add lime juice and cook 1 more minute. Serve.

PER SERVING
Calories: **394**
Fat: **22g**
Protein: **16g**

Sodium: **1,072mg**
Fiber: **4g**
Carbohydrates: **30g**
Sugar: **2g**

Chimichurri Steak Bites

Chimichurri sauce originated in Argentina. It's made from blended fresh herbs and garlic. This sauce uses cilantro, but parsley can be used instead if you prefer.

PREP TIME: 2 hours, 15 minutes*   **COOK TIME: 7 minutes**   **SERVES: 6**

1 large bunch cilantro

1 bunch scallions

1 medium jalapeño pepper, cut in half, some seeds removed

6 cloves garlic, peeled

$1/2$ cup plus 2 tablespoons olive oil, divided

3 tablespoons red wine vinegar

1 tablespoon soy sauce

$3/4$ teaspoon kosher salt

3 pounds sirloin steak, cut into bite-sized pieces

Avocado Chimichurri

To make a thick and creamy version of chimichurri, you can add a small ripe avocado. After setting aside $1/3$ cup of the chimichurri to marinate the steak, peel and pit an avocado. Add it to the food processor with the chimichurri, and blend until smooth.

1. To make chimichurri, in a food processor or blender, whirl cilantro, scallions, jalapeño, garlic, $1/2$ cup oil, vinegar, soy sauce, and salt until smooth, about 1 minute.

2. Put steak in a sealable 1-gallon plastic bag. Add $1/3$ cup of chimichurri. Massage bag until combined and marinate in refrigerator for 2–3 hours or overnight. Cover remaining chimichurri and store in refrigerator.

3. Preheat griddle to medium. Add remaining 2 tablespoons oil and then steak. Cook 5–7 minutes until steak is cooked to your preference.

4. Serve steak with remaining chimichurri on the side.

*Includes marinating time.

PER SERVING
Calories: **611**
Fat: **39g**
Protein: **50g**

Sodium: **408mg**
Fiber: **1g**
Carbohydrates: **3g**
Sugar: **1g**

The Ultimate Smash Burgers

Feel free to either add a seasoning blend or let these simple crispy-edged burgers shine as the star. Adding parchment paper between the burger press and the meat will prevent sticking.

PREP TIME: 10 minutes   **COOK TIME: 4 minutes**   **SERVES: 4**

$1\frac{1}{2}$ pounds 80/20 ground beef

$\frac{1}{2}$ teaspoon kosher salt, divided

$\frac{1}{4}$ teaspoon ground black pepper, divided

4 (1-ounce) slices **American cheese**

4 hamburger buns

12 pickle slices

$\frac{1}{2}$ cup burger sauce

$\frac{3}{4}$ cup shredded lettuce

Homemade Burger Sauce

Store-bought burger sauce is perfectly yummy, but here is an easy homemade recipe to try. In a small bowl, combine $\frac{1}{3}$ cup mayonnaise, 2 tablespoons ketchup, 1 tablespoon yellow mustard, 2 teaspoons pickle relish, and $\frac{1}{8}$ teaspoon each of garlic powder and paprika.

1. Divide and roll beef into 4 balls.
2. Preheat griddle to medium-high. Place beef balls on the Blackstone, spaced 6 inches apart. Use a burger press to smash each flat and thin, twisting slightly. Sprinkle $\frac{1}{4}$ teaspoon salt and $\frac{1}{8}$ teaspoon pepper on burgers. After 2 minutes, flip with spatulas.
3. Sprinkle remaining $\frac{1}{4}$ teaspoon salt and $\frac{1}{8}$ teaspoon pepper on burgers and top each with a slice of cheese. Cover with melting dome or lid for 1 more minute.
4. Place buns on the griddle, cut sides down, to toast for 20 seconds.
5. To assemble burgers, lay patties on bottom buns, then add pickles, burger sauce, lettuce, and top buns. Serve.

PER SERVING

Calories: **521**

Fat: **27g**

Protein: **30g**

Sodium: **1,333mg**

Fiber: **1g**

Carbohydrates: **31g**

Sugar: **9g**

Sausage and Pepper Quesadillas

This recipe will remind you of a sausage and pepper sandwich, only it's served in crisp tortillas. Of course, if you're craving a sandwich you could certainly serve the sausage and peppers from this recipe on toasted sub buns instead of in tortillas.

PREP TIME: **10 minutes**   COOK TIME: **14 minutes**   SERVES: **4**

2 tablespoons olive oil, divided

1 pound smoked sausage, sliced

1 medium yellow bell pepper, seeded and sliced

1 medium orange bell pepper, seeded and sliced

1 medium yellow onion, peeled and sliced

1 tablespoon Italian seasoning

1/2 teaspoon kosher salt

1/4 teaspoon ground black pepper

4 (10-inch) flour tortillas

16 (1-ounce) slices provolone cheese

1/2 cup sliced banana peppers

1 cup marinara sauce

1. Preheat griddle to medium. Add 1 tablespoon oil, sausage, bell peppers, onion, Italian seasoning, salt, and black pepper. Cook 8 minutes, mixing and tossing with spatulas. Remove and set aside. Scrape Blackstone and lower heat to medium-low.

2. Add remaining 1 tablespoon oil to griddle and lay tortillas flat. On one half of each tortilla, place 2 slices of cheese, then sausage and peppers, banana peppers, and 2 more slices of cheese. Use spatula to fold the empty side of each tortilla over the filled side, forming a half-moon shape.

3. Cook 2–3 minutes per side, or until cheese is melted and tortilla is crisped to your liking.

4. Serve with marinara sauce for dipping.

PER SERVING

Calories: **1,061**

Fat: **66g**

Protein: **50g**

Sodium: **3,136mg**

Fiber: **5g**

Carbohydrates: **54g**

Sugar: **9g**

Lazy Ravioli Lasagna

This is a quick version of the classic lasagna dish. No need to layer or assemble anything—just throw it all on the Blackstone and it's ready fast.

PREP TIME: 10 minutes   **COOK TIME: 10 minutes**   **SERVES: 6**

1 (20-ounce) bag frozen cheese ravioli, thawed

1 tablespoon olive oil

1 pound ground Italian sausage

1 medium yellow onion, peeled and diced

1 tablespoon Italian seasoning

$1/2$ teaspoon kosher salt

$1/4$ teaspoon ground black pepper

6 cloves garlic, peeled and minced

6 ounces spinach, chopped

1 (24-ounce) jar marinara sauce

2 cups shredded mozzarella cheese

8 basil leaves, sliced

Garlic Toast

You can make garlic toast on the Blackstone as the perfect side dish to go with this dinner. Scrape griddle and lower heat to medium-low. Add frozen slices of garlic toast for about 2–3 minutes per side or until toasted how you prefer. Thawing the garlic toast first will get them done even faster.

1. Preheat griddle to medium. Add ravioli to one side of the Blackstone, squirt 2 tablespoons water over it, and cover with a melting dome or lid. Add oil, sausage, and onion to other side of griddle. Cook everything 3 minutes, stirring ravioli halfway through the cooking time and adding 2 more tablespoons water before covering again. Break sausage apart with spatulas as it cooks.

2. Remove dome and set aside. Combine the ravioli with the sausage mixture and then add Italian seasoning, salt, pepper, garlic, and spinach. Cook 4 minutes, mixing everything together.

3. Pour marinara sauce over mixture, mix, and cook 2 more minutes. Sprinkle cheese on top and cover with melting dome or lid until cheese melts, about 1 minute.

4. Garnish with basil before serving.

PER SERVING
Calories: **570**
Fat: **35g**
Protein: **24g**
Sodium: **1,607mg**
Fiber: **3g**
Carbohydrates: **38g**
Sugar: **6g**

Smashed Lasagna Tacos

This recipe has all the yumminess of lasagna but is served in flour tortillas instead of with noodles. It is a fun, handheld way to enjoy lasagna!

PREP TIME: 10 minutes   **COOK TIME: 4 minutes**   **SERVES: 4**

1 pound ground Italian sausage

8 (6-inch) flour tortillas

4 ounces whole milk ricotta cheese

1 cup marinara sauce

1 cup shredded mozzarella cheese

$1/2$ teaspoon crushed red pepper flakes

6 basil leaves, sliced

1. Divide sausage and shape into 8 balls.
2. Preheat griddle to medium. Place sausage balls on griddle, spaced 6 inches apart. Cover each with a tortilla and use a burger press to flatten each one completely.
3. Cook 4 minutes, flip, and then top each with ricotta, marinara sauce, and mozzarella. Cook 1 minute or until mozzarella has melted. Garnish with red pepper flakes and basil before serving. Eat folded in half like a taco.

PER SERVING
Calories: **648**
Fat: **43g**
Protein: **25g**

Sodium: **1,792mg**
Fiber: **2g**
Carbohydrates: **37g**
Sugar: **5g**

Steak and Mushroom Burritos

Each of these burritos is a creamy, cheesy steak dinner wrapped up in an individual, handheld package. You can use mayonnaise in place of the horseradish for a milder version if you like.

PREP TIME: 15 minutes   **COOK TIME: 13 minutes**   **SERVES: 4**

2 tablespoons olive oil

8 ounces white mushrooms, sliced

1 medium yellow onion, peeled and diced

1 pound sirloin steak, cut into bite-sized pieces

1 teaspoon steak seasoning

1/4 teaspoon kosher salt

1/8 teaspoon ground black pepper

4 cloves garlic, peeled and minced

2 tablespoons Worcestershire sauce

4 (12-inch) flour tortillas

1/4 cup horseradish sauce

8 (1-ounce) slices provolone cheese

1. Preheat griddle to medium. Add oil, mushrooms, and onion. Cook 5 minutes, stirring with spatulas.

2. Add steak, steak seasoning, salt, pepper, garlic, and Worcestershire sauce. Cook 4 minutes, tossing with spatulas. Remove and set aside. Scrape Blackstone and lower heat to medium-low.

3. On a countertop or work surface, lay each tortilla flat. In the center of each, spread 1/4 of the horseradish sauce, then stack on 2 slices of cheese and some steak and mushrooms. Fold in sides and roll them up tightly.

4. Place burritos back on the griddle, starting with seam sides down, for 1–2 minutes per side until tortilla is crisped and browned to your liking.

PER SERVING
Calories: **855**
Fat: **37g**
Protein: **50g**
Sodium: **1,754mg**
Fiber: **7g**
Carbohydrates: **71g**
Sugar: **7g**

Garlic Herb Pork Tenderloin

This pork recipe has a simple marinade and seasoning. You could follow the same Blackstone cook time using store-bought, pre-seasoned pork tenderloin if desired. One benefit of cooking this on the flat top is the gorgeous sear that locks in the flavor and juices.

PREP TIME: 3 hours, 10 minutes*   **COOK TIME: 12 minutes**   **SERVES: 4**

1 (20-ounce) pork tenderloin

1/4 cup Italian dressing

1/2 tablespoon garlic herb seasoning

1/2 teaspoon kosher salt

1/4 teaspoon ground black pepper

1 tablespoon olive oil

1. Put pork tenderloin in a sealable 1-gallon plastic bag. Add Italian dressing, garlic herb seasoning, salt, and pepper. Massage bag until combined and then marinate in refrigerator 3 hours.

2. Preheat griddle to medium-high. Add oil and then pork. Cook 1 minute, flip with tongs, and cook 1 more minute.

3. Turn heat to medium-low and cover pork with melting dome or lid for 10 minutes. Remove dome to flip the pork a few times during the cooking time.

4. Let pork rest 5 minutes before slicing and serving.

*Includes marinating time.

PER SERVING
Calories: **173**
Fat: **7g**
Protein: **26g**
Sodium: **452mg**
Fiber: **0g**
Carbohydrates: **1g**
Sugar: **1g**

Beef Stroganoff

Beef stroganoff is often simmered in a pot, but you can also cook it on the Blackstone with huge success! Feel free to use diced steak in place of the ground beef if you prefer.

PREP TIME: **15 minutes**   COOK TIME: **10 minutes**   SERVES: **6**

1 (12-ounce) bag egg noodles

1 tablespoon olive oil

1 medium yellow onion, peeled and diced

8 ounces white mushrooms, sliced

1 pound 80/20 ground beef

$3/4$ teaspoon kosher salt

$1/4$ teaspoon ground black pepper

1 pint heavy cream

1 cup sour cream

2 tablespoons Worcestershire sauce

1 (1-ounce) packet onion soup seasoning

1 (4-ounce) container fried onions

1. Boil egg noodles according to package directions. Drain and rinse well with cold water.
2. Preheat griddle to medium. Add oil, yellow onion, mushrooms, beef, salt, and pepper. Cook 8 minutes, mixing and breaking up beef with spatulas.
3. Add cooked noodles, heavy cream, sour cream, Worcestershire sauce, onion soup seasoning, and half of fried onions. Cook 2 more minutes, mixing.
4. Serve with remaining fried onions sprinkled on top.

PER SERVING

Calories: **897**

Fat: **50g**

Protein: **29g**

Sodium: **822mg**

Fiber: **4g**

Carbohydrates: **73g**

Sugar: **7g**

Gochujang Pork Rice Bowls

This is a fabulous recipe to prepare ahead. Ground chicken can be used in place of the pork if you desire, and you also can add any other vegetables you like.

PREP TIME: 20 minutes   **COOK TIME: 10 minutes**   **SERVES: 4**

2 cups jasmine rice

2 tablespoons vegetable oil

1 pound ground pork

1 medium yellow onion, peeled and diced

1 medium red bell pepper, seeded and diced

1 cup shredded carrots

5 cloves garlic, peeled and minced

1 teaspoon grated ginger

3 tablespoons soy sauce

2 tablespoons gochujang

2 tablespoons honey

4 medium scallions, sliced

1/2 cup sriracha mayonnaise

1. Prepare rice according to package instructions.
2. Preheat griddle to medium. Add oil, pork, onion, pepper, and carrots and cook 3 minutes, breaking pork apart with spatulas.
3. Add garlic, ginger, soy sauce, gochujang, honey, and scallions. Cook 7 more minutes, mixing a few times.
4. Serve pork over rice and drizzle with sriracha mayonnaise.

PER SERVING
Calories: **850**
Fat: **41g**
Protein: **30g**
Sodium: **1,250mg**
Fiber: **5g**
Carbohydrates: **86g**
Sugar: **17g**

Fish and Seafood Main Dishes

Many people love seafood but shy away from cooking it at home because of the odor it can leave in the kitchen. With the Blackstone griddle, you can throw that apprehension out the window and enjoy all the health benefits that come from seafood and shellfish, without having to worry about odors. With your trusty griddle you no longer have to wait to dine out to enjoy your favorite seafood dishes.

In this chapter you are sure to find a wide variety of recipes to cure your craving for seafood. With terrific meals such as Scallops with Corn and Bacon, Shrimp Fried Rice, Cajun Mahi-Mahi Tacos, Tuna Croquettes, and Honey Mustard Salmon, this chapter covers a variety of tasty and delicious seafood dishes that you can assemble in minutes on your Blackstone griddle.

Shrimp Zucchini Kebabs

This dish is a light and healthy complete dinner on the Blackstone. It makes the perfect summer meal and is totally worthy of bringing out to wow your guests.

PREP TIME: **15 minutes**   COOK TIME: **8 minutes**   SERVES: **4**

1 pound jumbo shrimp, peeled and deveined

1 medium zucchini, cut into $1/2$-inch slices

1 medium yellow squash, cut into $1/2$-inch slices

1 pint grape tomatoes (whole)

1 pound andouille sausage, cut into $1/2$-inch slices

2 teaspoons seafood seasoning, divided

$1/2$ cup nonfat plain Greek yogurt

1 tablespoon lemon juice

2 tablespoons olive oil

1. On 8 skewers, assemble kebabs by alternating shrimp, vegetables, and sausage. Season them all over with 1 teaspoon seafood seasoning.

2. In a small bowl, stir yogurt, remaining 1 teaspoon seafood seasoning, and lemon juice until mixed.

3. Preheat griddle to medium. Add oil, place kebabs on the Blackstone. Cook 4 minutes, flip them, and cook 4 more minutes or until cooked through.

4. Serve kebabs with prepared dipping sauce on the side.

PER SERVING
Calories: **367**
Fat: **20g**
Protein: **38g**
Sodium: **2,250mg**
Fiber: **4g**
Carbohydrates: **11g**
Sugar: **5g**

Bang-Bang Salmon

You can adjust the spice level of the bang-bang sauce in this dish by adding more or less sriracha. The sugar in the sauce chars nicely on the salmon. If you prefer no char, skip the step of brushing the salmon prior to cooking.

PREP TIME: 5 minutes   **COOK TIME: 8 minutes**   **SERVES: 4**

$1/4$ cup mayonnaise

$1/4$ cup Thai sweet chili sauce

1 tablespoon sriracha

4 (5-ounce) salmon fillets (skin on)

$1/4$ teaspoon kosher salt

$1/8$ teaspoon ground black pepper

2 tablespoons olive oil

Bonus Recipe

This bang-bang sauce is also great for chicken kebabs! Cut up $1^1/2$ pounds boneless, skinless chicken thighs and arrange them on skewers. Season with kosher salt and pepper. Cook skewers on the griddle over medium heat with olive oil for 8–10 minutes, turning a few times. Brush on some sauce during the last half of the cooking time and serve with remaining sauce.

1. To make bang-bang sauce, in a small bowl, stir mayonnaise, sweet chili sauce, and sriracha until combined. Divide the mixture in half and set both portions aside.
2. Season top of salmon with salt and pepper and brush on half of prepared bang-bang sauce.
3. Preheat griddle to medium. Add oil and then salmon, skin-side up. Cook 8 minutes, flipping halfway through. Serve with remaining bang-bang sauce.

PER SERVING

Calories: **476**

Fat: **30g**

Protein: **29g**

Sodium: **610mg**

Fiber: **0g**

Carbohydrates: **10g**

Sugar: **10g**

Blackened Shrimp Lettuce Wraps

You could serve these in warm tortillas instead of lettuce leaves if preferred. However you wrap them, you can also top them with shredded cheese.

PREP TIME: 15 minutes   **COOK TIME: 10 minutes**   **SERVES: 4**

1 (5.3-ounce) container nonfat plain Greek yogurt

1 small avocado, pitted and scooped out of peel

1 tablespoon lime juice

$1/2$ teaspoon kosher salt, divided

2 tablespoons olive oil

1 medium yellow onion, peeled and sliced

1 medium red bell pepper, seeded and sliced

2 medium jalapeño peppers, seeded and sliced

4 cloves garlic, peeled and minced

1 pound jumbo shrimp, peeled and deveined

1 tablespoon blackened seasoning

1 head Boston lettuce, leaves separated

$1/2$ medium lime, cut into 4 wedges

1. To make avocado yogurt sauce, place yogurt, avocado, lime juice, and $1/4$ teaspoon salt in a food processor. Blend until smooth and set aside.

2. Preheat griddle to medium. Add oil, onion, peppers, and remaining $1/4$ teaspoon salt. Cook 5 minutes, stirring with spatulas.

3. Add garlic, shrimp, and blackened seasoning. Cook 5 more minutes, tossing.

4. Let mixture cool slightly. Spoon mixture into lettuce wraps. Drizzle with avocado yogurt sauce and serve with lime wedges.

PER SERVING
Calories: **235**
Fat: **11g**
Protein: **21g**

Sodium: **1,037mg**
Fiber: **4g**
Carbohydrates: **13g**
Sugar: **4g**

Pesto Shrimp Tortellini

This is a simple seafood and pasta dinner on the Blackstone. Sun-dried tomatoes and a topping of Parmesan cheese would both make nice flavor additions.

PREP TIME: 5 minutes   **COOK TIME: 11 minutes**   **SERVES: 4**

1 (20-ounce) bag frozen cheese tortellini, thawed

1 tablespoon olive oil

8 ounces spinach, chopped

1 pound jumbo shrimp, peeled and deveined

1/2 teaspoon kosher salt

1/4 teaspoon ground black pepper

2 cups Alfredo sauce

4 ounces pesto

1. Preheat griddle to medium. Add tortellini, squirt 2 tablespoons water over it, and cover with a melting dome or lid. Cook 4 minutes, mixing halfway through the cooking time and adding 2 more tablespoons water before covering again.

2. Remove dome and set aside. Add oil, spinach, shrimp, salt, and pepper. Cook 5 minutes, mixing with spatulas.

3. Add Alfredo sauce and pesto. Cook and mix 2 more minutes until combined. Serve right away.

PER SERVING

Calories: **725**

Fat: **40g**

Protein: **37g**

Sodium: **2,426mg**

Fiber: **10g**

Carbohydrates: **60g**

Sugar: **1g**

Sesame-Crusted Ahi Tuna

Depending on where you live, fresh ahi tuna can be a splurge. The griddle is by far the best way to get that sought-after sear and create a nice crust while still keeping the tuna perfectly medium rare in the center.

PREP TIME: 25 minutes* **COOK TIME: 5 minutes** **SERVES: 4**

3 tablespoons soy sauce

3 tablespoons honey

2 cloves garlic, peeled and minced

2 (8-ounce) ahi tuna steaks

3 tablespoons sesame seeds, mix of white and black

1/4 teaspoon kosher salt

2 tablespoons vegetable oil

4 cups mixed salad greens

1/2 cup sriracha mayonnaise

1. Put soy sauce, honey, and garlic in a shallow dish. Whisk until combined. Put tuna steaks in the dish and marinate 10 minutes per side.

2. Remove tuna from marinade and sprinkle sesame seeds and salt over both sides. Press into the tuna to help adhere.

3. Preheat griddle to medium-high. Add oil and then tuna. Cook 2–3 minutes per side until sesame seed crust is crisped to perfection.

4. Slice and serve over mixed greens, drizzled with sriracha mayonnaise.

*Includes marinating time.

PER SERVING
Calories: **398**
Fat: **29g**
Protein: **29g**
Sodium: **680mg**
Fiber: **1g**
Carbohydrates: **6g**
Sugar: **3g**

Honey Mustard Salmon

This simple salmon recipe is big on flavor. The sweet honey caramelizes on the griddle, creating a nice char. You could also add fresh herbs, such as rosemary, chives, or thyme, to the sauce if that sounds tasty.

PREP TIME: 5 minutes   **COOK TIME: 8 minutes**   **SERVES: 4**

4 tablespoons honey

4 tablespoons Dijon mustard

1 tablespoon soy sauce

$1/4$ teaspoon kosher salt

$1/8$ teaspoon ground black pepper

4 (5-ounce) salmon fillets (skin on)

2 tablespoons olive oil

1. To make honey mustard sauce, in a small bowl, mix honey, mustard, and soy sauce until combined. Divide the mixture in half and set both portions aside.
2. Sprinkle salt and pepper on top of salmon; brush half of honey mustard sauce over top.
3. Preheat griddle to medium. Add oil and then salmon. Cook 8 minutes, flipping halfway through the cooking time.
4. Serve with remaining honey mustard sauce.

PER SERVING

Calories: **435**

Fat: **22g**

Protein: **31g**

Sodium: **798mg**

Fiber: **0g**

Carbohydrates: **19g**

Sugar: **17g**

Lobster Tails with Lemon Garlic Butter

Lobster on the Blackstone is a decadent treat but very easy to prepare. You can add any fresh herbs that you like to the garlic butter.

PREP TIME: **5 minutes**   COOK TIME: **8 minutes**   SERVES: **2**

4 tablespoons unsalted butter

1 tablespoon lemon juice

4 cloves garlic, peeled and finely minced

1/4 teaspoon kosher salt

1/4 teaspoon paprika

2 (10-ounce) lobster tails

Splitting Lobster Tails

Most lobster tails are already split when you purchase them. If yours aren't, use sharp kitchen scissors to cut down the centers of the top shells and expose the meat. You could also ask at the seafood counter; they may be able to do the splitting for you.

1. To a small saucepan, add butter, lemon juice, garlic, salt, and paprika.
2. Preheat griddle to medium. Place saucepan on the Blackstone for 2 minutes, stirring as the butter melts. Move saucepan to the edge of the griddle to keep it warm.
3. Place lobster tails on griddle meat-side up, add 3 tablespoons water over top, and cover with a melting dome or lid for 6 minutes. Add more water under the dome a few times as it cooks.
4. When lobster is cooked, brush with garlic butter. Serve with extra garlic butter for dipping.

PER SERVING
Calories: **340**
Fat: **23g**
Protein: **28g**
Sodium: **932mg**
Fiber: **0g**
Carbohydrates: **3g**
Sugar: **0g**

Seafood "Boil"

Technically this recipe is not boiled, but it does have all the same ingredients as a seafood boil, and they cook perfectly on the flat top. For a cool presentation that's like the traditional seafood boil experience, serve this on a table lined with newspaper.

PREP TIME: **20 minutes**   COOK TIME: **12 minutes**   SERVES: **6**

$1^{1}/_{2}$ pounds small red potatoes

4 tablespoons unsalted butter, divided

4 ears corn, cut into thirds

1 pound jumbo shrimp, deveined (shells on)

$^{1}/_{2}$ pound lobster tails, split (shells on)

$^{1}/_{2}$ pound crab legs

1 pound smoked sausage, sliced

2 tablespoons lemon juice

1 tablespoon seafood seasoning

1. In a large pot of salted water, boil potatoes for 8 minutes or until fork-tender. Remove from water, cool slightly, and cut in half.

2. Preheat griddle to medium. Add 1 tablespoon butter, boiled potatoes, and corn. Cook 7 minutes, turning a few times with tongs.

3. Add remaining 3 tablespoons butter, shrimp, lobster, crab, sausage, lemon juice, and seafood seasoning. Cook 5 more minutes, turning and mixing a few times. Serve hot.

PER SERVING
Calories: **544**
Fat: **27g**
Protein: **31g**

Sodium: **1,667mg**
Fiber: **3g**
Carbohydrates: **37g**
Sugar: **6g**

Crab Cakes

This crab cake recipe comes from the author's dad and is a long-time family favorite that is now updated with a griddle twist to create that perfect sear.

PREP TIME: 30 minutes*   **COOK TIME: 15 minutes**   **SERVES: 4**

3 tablespoons olive oil, divided

1 medium yellow onion, peeled and finely diced

1 medium red bell pepper, seeded and finely diced

2 medium stalks celery, finely diced

3 cloves garlic, peeled and minced

1/2 teaspoon kosher salt

1/4 teaspoon ground black pepper

1 pound crabmeat

3/4 cup panko bread crumbs

2 large eggs, beaten

1/2 teaspoon seafood seasoning

1/2 cup rémoulade sauce

4 lemon wedges

Crabmeat

There are several options when purchasing crab. If you buy canned crab, be sure to drain the extra liquid well. Most seafood counters offer refrigerated crabmeat in many varieties, such as lump, claw, backfin, and white. Whichever type you use, be sure to check for shells before using.

1. Preheat griddle to medium. Add 1 tablespoon oil, onion, bell pepper, celery, garlic, salt, and black pepper. Cook 7 minutes, stirring a few times with spatulas. Turn Blackstone off, remove mixture, and transfer to a large bowl to cool.

2. Once vegetables have cooled, add crabmeat, panko, eggs, and seafood seasoning. Combine with your hands, then divide and shape into 8 patties. Let sit on countertop for 10 minutes.

3. Preheat griddle to medium. Add remaining 2 tablespoons oil and place patties on the Blackstone. Cook about 4 minutes per side or until golden brown.

4. Serve with rémoulade sauce and lemon wedges.

*Includes cooling and resting time.

PER SERVING

Calories: **421**	Sodium: **1,225mg**
Fat: **24g**	Fiber: **2g**
Protein: **25g**	Carbohydrates: **24g**
	Sugar: **6g**

Blackened Catfish Sandwiches

Inspired by a rather pricey and decadent restaurant favorite, here is a healthier catfish sandwich that you can enjoy at home (and it's very budget friendly!).

PREP TIME: 5 minutes   **COOK TIME: 10 minutes**   **SERVES: 4**

4 (6-ounce) catfish fillets

1 tablespoon all-purpose flour

1 teaspoon blackened seasoning

2 tablespoons olive oil

4 hamburger buns

1/2 cup shredded lettuce

1/2 cup rémoulade sauce

PER SERVING	
Calories: 512	Sodium: 622mg
Fat: 29g	Fiber: 1g
Protein: 30g	Carbohydrates: 26g
	Sugar: 5g

1. Pat catfish dry with paper towels and sprinkle flour and blackened seasoning on both sides, rubbing so the fish is evenly coated.
2. Preheat griddle to medium-low. Add oil and place catfish on the Blackstone. Cook 8–10 minutes or until crispy and golden brown. Place buns on griddle, cut sides down, for a few seconds until toasted to your liking.
3. Serve catfish on toasted buns with lettuce and rémoulade sauce.

Crab Rangoon Flatbreads

This recipe calls for real crab, but chopped imitation crabmeat is a fantastic substitution. Using whipped cream cheese makes the spreading so much easier.

PREP TIME: 5 minutes   **COOK TIME: 6 minutes**   **SERVES: 2**

2 (4-ounce) pieces naan

8 ounces whipped cream cheese

2 (4-ounce) cans crabmeat, drained

1/2 cup Thai sweet chili sauce

2 cups shredded mozzarella cheese

4 medium scallions, sliced

PER SERVING	
Calories: 1,129	Sodium: 3,575mg
Fat: 44g	Fiber: 3g
Protein: 58g	Carbohydrates: 113g
	Sugar: 49g

1. Preheat griddle to medium-low. Place naan on the Blackstone and cook 1 minute. Flip flatbreads and spread cream cheese on top, then add crabmeat, drizzle on half of sweet chili sauce (reserving half to top everything with later), and add mozzarella.
2. Cover with a melting dome or lid until cheese is melted, about 3–5 minutes.
3. Sprinkle with scallions and drizzle on remaining sweet chili sauce before serving.

Shrimp Fried Rice

Succulent shrimp with hibachi-style fried rice is sure to become one of your favorites. To take this to the next level, you could add some diced steak a few minutes before adding the shrimp for a fabulous surf and turf dinner.

PREP TIME: 5 minutes   **COOK TIME: 13 minutes**   **SERVES: 6**

2 tablespoons vegetable oil

6 cups cooked, cooled jasmine rice

1 medium yellow onion, peeled and diced

3 large eggs

1 (12-ounce) bag frozen diced peas and carrots, thawed

$1/2$ cup soy sauce, divided

3 tablespoons unsalted butter

4 cloves garlic, peeled and minced

$1^1/2$ pounds jumbo shrimp, peeled and deveined

1 tablespoon lemon juice

$1/2$ tablespoon white sesame seeds

$1/2$ cup yum-yum sauce

1. Preheat griddle to medium-high. Add oil, rice, onion, and eggs. Cook 3 minutes, mixing with spatulas and breaking apart eggs.

2. Add peas and carrots, most of soy sauce (reserving 2 tablespoons), butter, and garlic. Cook 5 minutes, stirring a few times. Add shrimp and remaining soy sauce to an empty part of the Blackstone and cook, tossing, for 2 minutes.

3. Combine shrimp and rice with spatulas and add lemon juice and sesame seeds over top. Cook 2–3 more minutes until rice is crisped to your preference. Serve right away with yum-yum sauce drizzled over top.

Homemade Yum-Yum Sauce

Fried rice is best served with yum-yum sauce. Store-bought is an easy option, but here's how to make your own: In a medium bowl, combine $1/2$ cup mayonnaise, 2 tablespoons ketchup, 1 teaspoon granulated sugar, and $1/8$ teaspoon each paprika and garlic powder.

PER SERVING	
Calories: **548**	Sodium: **2,013mg**
Fat: **24g**	Fiber: **4g**
Protein: **27g**	Carbohydrates: **56g**
	Sugar: **5g**

Cajun Mahi-Mahi Tacos

Fish tacos are light and fresh and so easy to make on the Blackstone griddle. You can also use a store-bought salad kit, minus the dressing packet, in place of the slaw for added texture, color, and variety of vegetables.

PREP TIME: **10 minutes**   COOK TIME: **10 minutes**   SERVES: **4**

4 (4-ounce) mahi-mahi fillets

1 teaspoon Cajun seasoning

2 cups coleslaw mix

$\frac{1}{2}$ cup tartar sauce

$\frac{1}{2}$ teaspoon Tabasco sauce

2 tablespoons vegetable oil, divided

12 (5-inch) corn tortillas

1 medium lime, cut into wedges

1. Pat mahi-mahi with paper towels to dry and then sprinkle all sides with Cajun seasoning.

2. To a medium bowl, add coleslaw, tartar sauce, and Tabasco. Toss until combined.

3. Preheat griddle to medium. Add 1 tablespoon oil and then mahi-mahi. Cook 4 minutes per side. Remove and set aside; scrape Blackstone if needed.

4. Add remaining 1 tablespoon oil to the griddle, then the tortillas. Cook 1–2 minutes, flipping a few times, until they are crisped to your liking.

5. Flake mahi-mahi into smaller pieces. Serve on tortillas with slaw and lime wedges to squeeze over top.

PER SERVING

Calories: **320**

Fat: **8g**

Protein: **26g**

Sodium: **218mg**

Fiber: **6g**

Carbohydrates: **35g**

Sugar: **2g**

Scallops with Corn and Bacon

This Blackstone dinner is quite a fancy treat. Be sure to remove the muscle from the side of each scallop to ensure a tender bite.

PREP TIME: **20 minutes**   COOK TIME: **12 minutes**   SERVES: **4**

4 slices bacon, cut into bite-sized pieces

3 ears corn, kernels cut off cobs

1 small red onion, peeled and diced

1 medium red bell pepper, seeded and diced

$1^{1}/_{2}$ teaspoons seafood seasoning, divided

1 pound jumbo scallops

1 tablespoon all-purpose flour

$^{1}/_{2}$ tablespoon olive oil

1. Preheat griddle to medium. Add bacon, corn, onion, pepper, and 1 teaspoon seafood seasoning. Cook 9 minutes, mixing with spatulas a few times.
2. Remove mixture and set aside. Scrape griddle and then turn heat to high. As griddle heats, pat scallops dry and sprinkle remaining $^{1}/_{2}$ teaspoon seafood seasoning on both sides.
3. Lightly coat scallops in flour. Add oil and scallops to griddle. Cook $1–1^{1}/_{2}$ minutes per side until seared golden brown. Remove and serve scallops over corn and bacon relish.

PER SERVING

Calories: **235**

Fat: **7g**

Protein: **21g**

Sodium: **860mg**

Fiber: **3g**

Carbohydrates: **23g**

Sugar: **7g**

Tuna Melt Sandwiches

The tuna melt is a classic comfort food that is very budget friendly and simple to prepare. The tuna salad can be prepared in advance and stored in the refrigerator.

PREP TIME: 15 minutes   **COOK TIME: 6 minutes**   **SERVES: 4**

3 (4-ounce) cans tuna packed in water, drained well

1/2 cup mayonnaise

1/2 cup minced celery

1/4 cup chopped scallions

2 tablespoons sweet pickle relish

1 tablespoon yellow mustard

8 (1-ounce) slices white sandwich bread

8 (1-ounce) slices American cheese

3 tablespoons unsalted butter

1. In a medium bowl, add tuna, mayonnaise, celery, scallions, relish, and mustard. Stir until combined.

2. On a tray or countertop, lay down 4 slices of bread. Add a cheese slice to each, then some tuna salad, another slice of cheese, and a top slice of bread.

3. Preheat griddle to medium-low. Add butter and, once melted, place sandwiches on the Blackstone. Cook 2–3 minutes per side or until golden brown. Serve right away.

PER SERVING

Calories: **657**

Fat: **38g**

Protein: **35g**

Sodium: **1,670mg**

Fiber: **2g**

Carbohydrates: **38g**

Sugar: **8g**

Caribbean Jerk Salmon Burgers

Serve these tasty burgers with any toppings you like, such as lettuce, cilantro, jalapeños, diced mango or pineapple, Caribbean jerk sauce, or rémoulade sauce.

PREP TIME: 25 minutes*   **COOK TIME: 10 minutes**   **SERVES: 4**

1 pound salmon, skin removed, cut into 2-inch pieces

$1/4$ cup chopped scallions

$1/4$ cup panko bread crumbs

2 tablespoons soy sauce

2 tablespoons Caribbean jerk seasoning

1 large egg, beaten

2 cloves garlic, peeled and finely minced

2 tablespoons olive oil

4 hamburger buns

1. Put salmon in a food processor and pulse a few times until it's blended together but is not completely smooth. Transfer to a medium bowl.
2. Add scallions, panko, soy sauce, jerk seasoning, egg, and garlic. Combine with your hands and form 4 patties. Place on a tray and let sit on the countertop for 10 minutes.
3. Preheat griddle to medium-low. Add oil and cook patties for about 5 minutes per side or until golden brown.
4. Place buns, cut sides down, on griddle for a few seconds until toasted to your liking.
5. Serve salmon burgers on toasted buns.

*Includes resting time.

PER SERVING

Calories: **451**
Fat: **20g**
Protein: **30g**

Sodium: **966mg**
Fiber: **1g**
Carbohydrates: **28g**
Sugar: **3g**

Lemon Dill Catfish

This recipe creates a simple but delicious meal that is ready in just minutes. You could also add some asparagus, kale, or broccoli to this dish, as they would all have the same cook time on the griddle.

PREP TIME: 10 minutes　　**COOK TIME: 10 minutes**　　**SERVES: 4**

4 (6-ounce) catfish fillets

1 teaspoon seafood seasoning

3 tablespoons unsalted butter, melted

2 tablespoons lemon juice

2 tablespoons chopped fresh dill

1. Pat catfish dry with paper towels and sprinkle both sides with seafood seasoning.
2. In a small bowl, place butter, lemon juice, and dill and stir until combined.
3. Preheat griddle to medium-low. Add half of lemon-dill butter and then catfish. Cook 8–10 minutes total, depending on thickness of the fish, flipping halfway through the cooking time.
4. Serve with remaining lemon and dill butter drizzled over the catfish.

PER SERVING

Calories: **260**

Fat: **15g**

Protein: **26g**

Sodium: **307mg**

Fiber: **0g**

Carbohydrates: **0g**

Sugar: **0g**

Spicy Lobster Quesadillas

You can use chopped shrimp or crabmeat in this recipe if you prefer. And if you aren't a fan of spice, just leave out the jalapeño and use Monterey jack cheese in place of the pepper jack.

PREP TIME: 5 minutes   **COOK TIME: 10 minutes**   **SERVES: 4**

2 tablespoons olive oil, divided

2 medium jalapeño peppers, sliced

1$\frac{1}{2}$ pounds lobster meat, cooked and chopped

$\frac{1}{2}$ teaspoon seafood seasoning

4 (10-inch) flour tortillas

16 (1-ounce) slices pepper jack cheese

1. Preheat griddle to medium-low. Add 1 tablespoon oil and jalapeños. Cook 2 minutes, then add lobster and seafood seasoning. Cook 2 more minutes, mixing with spatulas. Remove and set aside. Scrape Blackstone.

2. Add remaining 1 tablespoon oil to griddle and lay tortillas flat on the griddle. On one half of each tortilla, put 2 slices of cheese, then evenly add lobster and jalapeños on top, then add 2 more slices of cheese per tortilla. Use spatulas to fold empty side of each tortilla over the filled side, forming a half-moon shape.

3. Cook 2–3 minutes per side or until cheese is melted and tortillas are crisped to your taste before serving.

PER SERVING

Calories: **831**

Fat: **43g**

Protein: **66g**

Sodium: **2,087mg**

Fiber: **2g**

Carbohydrates: **38g**

Sugar: **3g**

Ginger Wasabi Salmon

The sesame crust on the salmon gives this dish a nice texture. Make sure you use wasabi *sauce* in this recipe and not the much more intense wasabi *paste*. If you cannot find wasabi sauce, simply mix a little wasabi paste with some mayonnaise. Serve with grilled vegetables.

PREP TIME: 10 minutes   **COOK TIME: 9 minutes**   **SERVES: 4**

2 tablespoons soy sauce

2 tablespoons honey

2 tablespoons wasabi sauce

$1/2$ tablespoon grated ginger

4 (5-ounce) salmon fillets (skin on)

$1/4$ teaspoon kosher salt

2 tablespoons sesame seeds, mix of white and black

2 tablespoons vegetable oil

1. Place soy sauce, honey, wasabi sauce, and ginger in a small bowl. Stir until combined. Divide mixture in half and set both portions aside.
2. Brush half of this sauce on salmon. Sprinkle salt and sesame seeds on top.
3. Preheat griddle to medium. Add oil and then salmon, sesame-crusted-side down. Cook 8–9 minutes, flipping halfway through the cooking time, until salmon is seared and skin is crisp. Serve with remaining sauce.

PER SERVING
Calories: **408**
Fat: **23g**
Protein: **30g**

Sodium: **660mg**
Fiber: **1g**
Carbohydrates: **10g**
Sugar: **9g**

Tuna Croquettes

Here is a family-friendly dinner that is also easy on your budget! You can use canned salmon in place of the tuna if desired. Feel free to add more oil to the griddle if you find you need it after flipping the croquettes.

PREP TIME: 25 minutes*   **COOK TIME: 8 minutes**   **SERVES: 4**

2 (4-ounce) cans tuna packed in water, drained

3/4 cup panko bread crumbs, divided

2 large eggs, beaten

3 medium scallions, chopped

1/2 tablespoon Dijon mustard

1/2 teaspoon kosher salt

1/4 teaspoon ground black pepper

2 tablespoons olive oil

1/2 cup tartar sauce

4 lemon wedges

1. In a medium bowl, place tuna, 1/3 cup panko, eggs, scallions, mustard, salt, and pepper. Combine with your hands and shape into 8 patties. Place on a tray and let sit on countertop for 10 minutes.
2. Place remaining panko on a medium plate. Lightly coat each croquette in the panko on both sides.
3. Preheat griddle to medium. Add oil and place croquettes on the Blackstone for about 4 minutes per side or until cooked through and golden brown.
4. Serve with tartar sauce and lemon wedges.

*Includes resting time.

PER SERVING

Calories: **239**

Fat: **10g**

Protein: **19g**

Sodium: **590mg**

Fiber: **0g**

Carbohydrates: **17g**

Sugar: **1g**

Trout with Chive Butter

You can make this same recipe with any fish you like. Fattier fishes like salmon and tuna may take a bit longer to cook than trout does. Leaner fishes—tilapia, halibut, and catfish, for example—will have cooking times more similar to trout.

PREP TIME: 10 minutes   **COOK TIME: 10 minutes**   **SERVES: 4**

4 tablespoons unsalted butter, melted

2 tablespoons chopped chives

3 cloves garlic, peeled and finely minced

4 (6-ounce) trout fillets

1 teaspoon seafood seasoning

4 lemon wedges

About Trout

Trout comes in several varieties, the most popular being rainbow, golden, and steelhead. A mild fish, usually white or slightly pink, with a delicate taste, it's one of the healthiest types of fish, high in calcium, protein, potassium, magnesium, and omega-3 fatty acids.

1. In a small bowl, place butter, chives, and garlic. Stir until combined.
2. Pat trout dry with paper towels and season both sides with seafood seasoning.
3. Preheat griddle to medium-low. Add half of chive butter to the Blackstone and then trout. Cook 8–10 minutes total, depending on thickness of trout, flipping halfway through the cooking time.
4. Serve trout with remaining chive butter and lemon wedges.

PER SERVING
Calories: **343**
Fat: **19g**
Protein: **36g**
Sodium: **229mg**
Fiber: **0g**
Carbohydrates: **1g**
Sugar: **0g**

Tilapia with Citrus Gremolata

Gremolata is a condiment made of blended fresh parsley, lemon, and garlic that brings a bright freshness to meat, seafood, and vegetables.

PREP TIME: 15 minutes   **COOK TIME: 8 minutes**   **SERVES: 6**

1 large bunch flat-leaf parsley, bottom 3 inches of stems removed

1 teaspoon lemon zest

1 teaspoon orange zest

3 tablespoons lemon juice

3 tablespoons orange juice

3 cloves garlic, peeled

$1/3$ cup plus 2 tablespoons olive oil, divided

6 (6-ounce) tilapia fillets

$1/2$ teaspoon kosher salt

$1/4$ teaspoon ground black pepper

1. In a food processor or blender, place parsley, lemon and orange zest and juice, garlic, and $1/3$ cup oil. Blend until smooth, about 1 minute.
2. Pat tilapia dry with paper towels and season both sides with salt and pepper.
3. Preheat griddle to medium-low. Add remaining 2 tablespoons oil and place tilapia on Blackstone. Cook 4 minutes, flip with spatulas, add a spoonful of gremolata over each fillet, and cook 4 more minutes.
4. Serve with remaining gremolata over top.

Freezing Gremolata

If you have leftover gremolata from this recipe you can freeze it in a covered container for up to 3 months. Just thaw on the countertop before serving. You can also make the gremolata in big batches when you have extra time and then freeze it in smaller containers to use in several meals.

PER SERVING

Calories: **307**

Fat: **17g**

Protein: **34g**

Sodium: **249mg**

Fiber: **0g**

Carbohydrates: **2g**

Sugar: **1g**

CHAPTER 8

Vegetarian Main Dishes

Whether you are a practicing vegetarian or just someone interested in having a few meatless meals during the week, this chapter has you covered. In this chapter you'll find so many amazing options for meatless meals, one is sure to hit the spot. From Mediterranean Vegetable Naan Foldovers and Cheesy Spaghetti Squash to Bang-Bang Ramen Noodles, Goat Cheese Vegetable Sliders, and Potsticker Stir-Fry, these meatless dishes will have you wanting more. The best part is that cooking vegetarian mainstays like tofu and vegetables on your Blackstone griddle takes only a fraction of the time it would take in a traditional oven. So you get dinner on the table in no time and a happy and healthy family with some new favorite dishes!

Potsticker Stir-Fry

This dish is a hearty meal with bold Asian flavors and fresh vegetables, and the leftovers (if there are any!) reheat very well. For a spicy kick, drizzle some sriracha on top or serve with yum-yum sauce for dipping.

PREP TIME: 15 minutes   **COOK TIME: 10 minutes**   **SERVES: 6**

2 tablespoons vegetable oil

1 medium red bell pepper, seeded and sliced

1 medium yellow bell pepper, seeded and sliced

1 cup shredded carrots

8 ounces white mushrooms, sliced

1/4 teaspoon kosher salt

1 (24-ounce) package frozen vegetable potstickers (with sauce packet), thawed

6 medium scallions, cut into 2-inch pieces

6 cloves garlic, peeled and minced

1/2 tablespoon grated ginger

3 tablespoons soy sauce

3 tablespoons hoisin sauce

1. Preheat griddle to medium. Add oil and put peppers, carrots, mushrooms, and salt on one side of griddle. Place potstickers on the other side and squirt 2 tablespoons water over them. Cover potstickers with a melting dome or lid.

2. Cook everything 6 minutes. During cooking, stir vegetables a few times with spatulas and remove melting dome a few times to flip potstickers and add more water before covering again.

3. After 6 minutes, remove dome and set aside. Combine potstickers and vegetables and add scallions, garlic, and ginger. Cook 2 minutes, mixing everything together with spatulas.

4. Add soy sauce, hoisin sauce, and sauce packet from potsticker package. Cook 2 more minutes, mixing. Serve warm.

PER SERVING
Calories: **286**
Fat: **10g**
Protein: **9g**
Sodium: **1,418mg**
Fiber: **3g**
Carbohydrates: **41g**
Sugar: **11g**

Pizza-Style Portobello Mushrooms

Though these cheesy, saucy mushrooms are delicious on their own, you could also add any vegetable toppings you like. In addition, you could amp up the cheese factor and add some goat cheese crumbles to the mozzarella.

PREP TIME: **5 minutes**   COOK TIME: **10 minutes**   SERVES: **4**

4 large portobello mushroom caps

2 tablespoons olive oil

1/2 teaspoon kosher salt

1/4 teaspoon ground black pepper

1 cup pizza sauce

4 cups shredded mozzarella cheese

1/2 teaspoon Italian seasoning

1/4 teaspoon garlic powder

1. Brush mushrooms on both sides with oil and season with salt and pepper.
2. Preheat griddle to medium. Place mushrooms on the Blackstone, stem sides down, and cook 5 minutes.
3. Flip mushrooms and add pizza sauce, cheese, Italian seasoning, and garlic powder. Cover with melting dome or lid, cook 5 more minutes, and serve.

PER SERVING

Calories: **359**

Fat: **21g**

Protein: **24g**

Sodium: **1,053mg**

Fiber: **2g**

Carbohydrates: **16g**

Sugar: **6g**

Mediterranean Vegetable Naan Foldovers

This recipe's healthy mix of flat top griddle–cooked vegetables is delightful tucked inside a warm and toasty round of naan. If you're looking for a different serving option, it's also fabulous over cooked couscous or quinoa.

PREP TIME: 10 minutes   **COOK TIME: 10 minutes**   **SERVES: 4**

2 tablespoons olive oil

1 medium red onion, peeled and diced

1 pint grape tomatoes (whole)

1 small eggplant, diced

5 cloves garlic, peeled and minced

2 teaspoons dried oregano

1/2 teaspoon kosher salt

1/4 teaspoon ground black pepper

1 (15-ounce) can chickpeas, drained and rinsed

2 tablespoons balsamic vinegar

8 pieces mini naan

1/2 cup crumbled feta cheese

1. Preheat griddle to medium. Add oil, onion, tomatoes, eggplant, garlic, oregano, salt, and pepper. Cook 7 minutes, mixing and tossing with spatulas.
2. Add chickpeas and vinegar. Cook and stir 3 more minutes. Place mini naan on the Blackstone to warm for a few seconds.
3. Assemble foldovers by adding vegetables to mini naan. Top with cheese before serving.

About Chickpeas

Chickpeas are also known as garbanzo beans and are in the legume family. They are high in iron, folate, magnesium, fiber, and protein, which gives multiple health benefits, such as heart health, lowering blood sugar, weight management, and boosting brain health.

PER SERVING

Calories: **408**

Fat: **14g**

Protein: **15g**

Sodium: **951mg**

Fiber: **11g**

Carbohydrates: **58g**

Sugar: **15g**

Garden Vegetable Fettuccine Alfredo

This dish is perfect for when you have garden-fresh vegetables. You can use store-bought or homemade Alfredo sauce. It is also very good topped with some vegetarian Parmesan cheese.

PREP TIME: 15 minutes   **COOK TIME: 10 minutes**   **SERVES: 6**

12 ounces fettuccine

2 tablespoons olive oil

1 medium zucchini, cut into 1-inch pieces

1 medium yellow squash, cut into 1-inch pieces

8 ounces cherry tomatoes (whole)

3 ears corn, kernels cut off cobs

3/4 teaspoon kosher salt

1/2 teaspoon ground black pepper

6 cloves garlic, peeled and minced

2 cups Alfredo sauce

1. Boil fettuccine according to the package directions. Drain and rinse well with cold water.
2. Preheat griddle to medium. Add oil, zucchini, squash, tomatoes, corn, salt, and pepper. Cook 6 minutes, stirring with spatulas.
3. Add garlic and cook 2 more minutes. Add cooked pasta and Alfredo sauce; mix with spatulas another 2 minutes. Serve warm.

Homemade Alfredo Sauce

Jarred Alfredo sauce is good, but homemade is so easy to make. Put 3 tablespoons butter in a saucepan over medium heat. Once it melts, pour in 1 1/2 cups heavy cream and season with kosher salt and pepper. Once it starts bubbling let it simmer for 5 minutes, stirring a few times. Then stir in 1 1/2 cups shredded vegetarian Parmesan cheese.

PER SERVING
Calories: **463**
Fat: **20g**
Protein: **14g**

Sodium: **774mg**
Fiber: **5g**
Carbohydrates: **60g**
Sugar: **7g**

Sweet Potatoes with Kale and Quinoa

This gorgeous, fresh dish has vibrant colors and tastes just as yummy as it looks. Quinoa is a whole grain that's packed with vitamins, protein, and fiber, making this a very filling and healthy meatless meal.

PREP TIME: **15 minutes**   COOK TIME: **12 minutes**   SERVES: **4**

$1/2$ cup quinoa

2 tablespoons olive oil, divided

1 medium sweet potato (with skin), diced

1 large bunch kale, stems removed, roughly chopped

$1/2$ teaspoon ground cumin

$1/2$ teaspoon kosher salt

$1/4$ teaspoon ground black pepper

$1/2$ cup dried cranberries

2 tablespoons lemon juice

$1/4$ cup crumbled feta cheese

1. In a saucepan, combine quinoa with 1 cup water. Bring to a boil, then simmer, uncovered, until liquid is absorbed, about 12 minutes. Cover and set aside.

2. Preheat griddle to medium. Add 1 tablespoon oil and sweet potato, squirt some water over top, and then cover with a melting dome or lid. Cook 8 minutes, lifting lid a few times to stir with spatulas and add more water before covering again.

3. Add remaining 1 tablespoon oil, kale, cumin, salt, and pepper. Cook 3 more minutes, tossing with spatulas.

4. Add quinoa, cranberries, and lemon juice. Cook 1 more minute, mixing everything together. Serve topped with cheese.

PER SERVING   Sodium: **361mg**
Calories: **245**   Fiber: **5g**
Fat: **8g**   Carbohydrates: **38g**
Protein: **6g**   Sugar: **13g**

Pierogi and Peppers

This colorful mix of peppers and soft dumplings is a cheesy and creamy comfort food meal on the Blackstone.

PREP TIME: **15 minutes**   COOK TIME: **13 minutes**   SERVES: **4**

1 (16-ounce) package frozen cheese pierogi, thawed

2 tablespoons olive oil

1 medium red bell pepper, seeded and sliced

1 medium yellow bell pepper, seeded and sliced

1 medium orange bell pepper, seeded and sliced

1 medium red onion, peeled and sliced

6 cloves garlic, peeled and minced

1 tablespoon Italian seasoning

1/2 teaspoon kosher salt

1/4 teaspoon ground black pepper

1 (16-ounce) jar Alfredo sauce

1 cup shredded vegetarian Parmesan cheese

1. Preheat griddle to medium. Add pierogi on one side of the Blackstone, squirt with 2 tablespoons water, and cover with a melting dome or lid for 3 minutes. Halfway through the cooking time, flip pierogi with tongs and add 2 more tablespoons water before covering again.

2. While the pierogi are cooking, on the other side of griddle, add oil, bell peppers, and onion. Cook 3 minutes, mixing a few times with spatulas.

3. Combine pierogi and vegetables and add garlic, Italian seasoning, salt, and black pepper. Mix everything together with spatulas and cook 6 more minutes.

4. Pour on Alfredo sauce and sprinkle on cheese, combine with spatulas, and cook 1 more minute before serving.

What Are Pierogi?

Pierogi are half circle–shaped dumplings. Pierogi is the Polish word for filled dumplings. Pierogi can be filled with a variety of ingredients, such as cheese, potatoes, sauerkraut, or onions.

PER SERVING

Calories: **564**

Fat: **33g**

Protein: **19g**

Sodium: **1,801mg**

Fiber: **3g**

Carbohydrates: **49g**

Sugar: **5g**

Tofu Egg Roll Bowls

Tofu is a fabulous vegetarian ingredient that is low in calories, an excellent source of protein, and high in many essential vitamins and minerals.

PREP TIME: 10 minutes   **COOK TIME: 10 minutes**   **SERVES: 4**

1 tablespoon vegetable oil

1 pound extra-firm tofu, diced

1 (8-ounce) bag coleslaw mix

1 cup shredded carrots

4 medium scallions, sliced

5 cloves garlic, peeled and minced

1/3 cup soy sauce

1 tablespoon lime juice

1/4 cup yum-yum sauce

1. Preheat griddle to medium. Add oil and tofu. Cook 2 minutes, tossing with spatulas.
2. Add coleslaw, carrots, scallions, and garlic. Mix and cook 5 more minutes.
3. Add soy sauce and lime juice. Mix everything together and cook 2–3 more minutes until vegetables are cooked to your liking.
4. Serve in bowls with yum-yum sauce drizzled on top.

Pressing Your Tofu

Tofu contains a fair amount of water. Pressing your tofu to remove excess liquid will create a firmer, chewier texture and make it easier to cook the exterior to crispy perfection. Pressing out liquid also makes room for the tofu to soak up other delicious flavors. To press, before dicing, place the block of tofu on a few paper towels, and place a few more paper towels on top. Set something heavy, such as a book or a cast iron skillet, on top for about 20 minutes.

PER SERVING
Calories: **293**
Fat: **17g**
Protein: **16g**
Sodium: **1,323mg**
Fiber: **7g**
Carbohydrates: **22g**
Sugar: **11g**

Cheesy Spaghetti Squash

This dinner for two is a lot of fun to make on the Blackstone. If your squash is on the larger side, microwave it for an extra minute, and it may need a little more time on the griddle.

PREP TIME: **10 minutes**   COOK TIME: **32 minutes**   SERVES: **2**

1 small spaghetti squash

1 tablespoon olive oil

1/2 teaspoon kosher salt

1/4 teaspoon ground black pepper

1/2 tablespoon Italian seasoning

1/2 teaspoon garlic powder

2 cups marinara sauce

2 cups shredded mozzarella cheese

1. Poke a few holes in squash with the tip of a sharp knife. Microwave for 7 minutes.
2. Cut squash in half lengthwise. Scoop out seeds, drizzle oil over the cut side, and season with salt and pepper.
3. Preheat griddle to medium. Place squash cut-side down on griddle, add 3 tablespoons water over top, and cover with melting dome or lid for 14 minutes. Add more water a few times during the cooking time.
4. Flip squash, add more water, cover again, and cook another 12–14 minutes until tender.
5. Sprinkle with Italian seasoning and garlic powder. Fill each squash cavity with marinara sauce and sprinkle cheese on top. Cover and cook another 3–4 minutes or until cheese is melted, then serve.

PER SERVING

Calories: **567**

Fat: **32g**

Protein: **27g**

Sodium: **1,962mg**

Fiber: **6g**

Carbohydrates: **40g**

Sugar: **18g**

Kale, White Beans, and Mushrooms

A hearty meatless meal packed with superfoods and yumminess. This complete stir-fried Blackstone dinner is extra good when topped with feta or goat cheese crumbles.

PREP TIME: 15 minutes   **COOK TIME: 10 minutes**   **SERVES: 4**

2 tablespoons olive oil

1 medium red onion, peeled and sliced

8 ounces baby portobello mushrooms, sliced

$1/2$ teaspoon kosher salt

$1/4$ teaspoon ground black pepper

6 cloves garlic, peeled and minced

1 tablespoon Italian seasoning

1 large bunch kale, stems removed, roughly chopped

1 (15.5-ounce) can white beans, drained and rinsed

1. Preheat griddle to medium. Add oil, onion, mushrooms, salt, and pepper. Cook 6 minutes, stirring with spatulas.

2. Add garlic, Italian seasoning, kale, and beans. Cook 4 more minutes, tossing. Serve warm.

PER SERVING

Calories: **224**

Fat: **6g**

Protein: **12g**

Sodium: **510mg**

Fiber: **8g**

Carbohydrates: **34g**

Sugar: **5g**

Street Corn Chilaquiles

Chilaquiles are a traditional Mexican breakfast, but here they are transformed into a delicious dinner with the addition of street corn ingredients. It is highly recommended that you garnish this dish with cilantro and add some sweet pickled red onions.

PREP TIME: 10 minutes   **COOK TIME: 12 minutes**   **SERVES: 6**

$1/3$ cup mayonnaise

$1/3$ cup sour cream

1 tablespoon lime juice

2 teaspoons chili powder

1 teaspoon garlic powder

1 tablespoon vegetable oil

3 ears corn, kernels cut off cobs

1 medium yellow onion, peeled and diced

$1/4$ teaspoon kosher salt

6 cups tortilla chips

1 (16-ounce) jar salsa verde

1 cup shredded Cheddar cheese

$1/2$ cup crumbled cotija cheese

1. To make sauce, put mayonnaise, sour cream, lime juice, chili powder, and garlic powder in a small bowl. Stir until combined. Set aside.
2. Preheat griddle to medium. Add oil, corn, onion, and salt. Cook 8 minutes, tossing with spatulas.
3. Add chips and salsa verde. Gently mix with spatulas and cook 3 minutes. Top with Cheddar and cotija and cover with melting dome or lid until cheese is melted, about 1 minute.
4. Serve drizzled with prepared sauce.

PER SERVING

Calories: **467**

Fat: **28g**

Protein: **11g**

Sodium: **1,089mg**

Fiber: **3g**

Carbohydrates: **37g**

Sugar: **10g**

Caprese Tortellini

You will fall in love with this twist on the caprese salad transformed into a cheesy pasta dinner. You can also mix in some pesto or top this dish with fresh basil if desired. Also, feel free to use burrata or fresh mozzarella in place of the shredded mozzarella.

PREP TIME: 5 minutes   **COOK TIME: 10 minutes**   **SERVES: 4**

1 (20-ounce) bag frozen cheese tortellini, thawed

1 tablespoon olive oil

1 pint grape tomatoes (whole)

8 ounces spinach, chopped

6 cloves garlic, peeled and minced

2 teaspoons Italian seasoning

1/2 teaspoon kosher salt

1/4 teaspoon ground black pepper

1/4 cup balsamic vinegar

1 1/2 cups shredded mozzarella cheese

1/2 cup shredded vegetarian Parmesan cheese

1. Preheat griddle to medium. Add tortellini, squirt with 2 tablespoons water, and cover with a melting dome or lid for 4 minutes. Flip halfway through the cooking time, adding 2 more tablespoons water before covering again.

2. Add oil, tomatoes, spinach, garlic, Italian seasoning, salt, and pepper. Cook 5 minutes, tossing with spatulas.

3. Add vinegar and cheeses and cook 1 more minute, mixing everything together. Serve right away.

PER SERVING
Calories: **504**
Fat: **16g**
Protein: **28g**
Sodium: **1,118mg**
Fiber: **11g**
Carbohydrates: **63g**
Sugar: **7g**

Pesto Sun-Dried Tomato Quesadillas

You can make all four of these quesadillas at once on the large Blackstone cook space. Try adding white beans or tofu for a boost of protein if you are so inclined.

PREP TIME: **5 minutes**   COOK TIME: **6 minutes**   SERVES: **4**

1 tablespoon olive oil

4 (10-inch) flour tortillas

3 cups shredded mozzarella cheese

$1/2$ cup pesto

4 ounces sliced sun-dried tomatoes

4 ounces crumbled feta cheese

1. Preheat griddle to medium-low. Add oil and lay each tortilla flat on griddle.
2. On one half of each tortilla, add some mozzarella, pesto, sun-dried tomatoes, feta, and then more mozzarella. Use spatula to fold empty sides of tortillas over filled sides, forming half-moon shapes.
3. Cook 2–3 minutes per side or until cheese is melted and tortillas are crisped. Serve.

PER SERVING

Calories: **676**

Fat: **34g**

Protein: **30g**

Sodium: **1,579mg**

Fiber: **6g**

Carbohydrates: **62g**

Sugar: **16g**

Pesto Tomato Flatbreads

These flatbreads are fresh and simple, grilled to perfection on the Blackstone. Try making these with garden tomatoes. You can substitute fresh mozzarella for the burrata.

PREP TIME: **5 minutes**   COOK TIME: **6 minutes**   SERVES: **2**

2 (4-ounce) flatbreads

$1/2$ cup pesto

8 ounces burrata, cut into 2-inch pieces

1 pint cherry tomatoes, cut in half

$1/2$ teaspoon kosher salt

$1/4$ teaspoon ground black pepper

4 basil leaves, sliced

1. Preheat griddle to medium-low. Place flatbreads on the Blackstone for 1 minute and then flip them over.
2. Spread pesto on flatbreads and top with burrata, tomatoes, salt, and pepper. Cover with melting dome or lid for 3–5 minutes or until cheese is melted.
3. Remove from griddle, let cool slightly, cut, and serve with basil sprinkled on top.

PER SERVING

Calories: **932**

Fat: **56g**

Protein: **35g**

Sodium: **2,321mg**

Fiber: **5g**

Carbohydrates: **67g**

Sugar: **9g**

Vegetable Hummus Wraps

These wraps are packed full of perfectly cooked vegetables and then seared on the Blackstone for an added crisp texture. If you like, you can use high-fiber, low-carb wraps in place of flour tortillas.

PREP TIME: 15 minutes   **COOK TIME: 12 minutes**   **SERVES: 2**

1 tablespoon olive oil

8 ounces baby portobello mushrooms, sliced

1 medium red onion, peeled and sliced

1 medium red bell pepper, seeded and sliced

1/4 teaspoon kosher salt

1/8 teaspoon ground black pepper

6 ounces spinach, chopped

4 cloves garlic, peeled and minced

1 teaspoon dried oregano

2 tablespoons balsamic vinegar

1/2 cup hummus

1/2 cup feta cheese crumbles

2 (12-inch) flour tortillas

1. Preheat griddle to medium. Add oil, mushrooms, onion, bell pepper, salt, and black pepper. Cook 5 minutes, stirring with spatulas.
2. Add spinach, garlic, oregano, and vinegar. Mix and cook another 3 minutes.
3. Remove mixture from the Blackstone. To assemble wraps, spread hummus and cheese in the center of each tortilla. Add cooked vegetables and then fold in the sides and wrap them tightly.
4. Place wraps back on griddle seam-side down. Cook 1–2 minutes per side until crisped and browned to your preference before serving.

PER SERVING

Calories: **695**

Fat: **25g**

Protein: **26g**

Sodium: **1,728mg**

Fiber: **12g**

Carbohydrates: **92g**

Sugar: **15g**

Balsamic Vegetable Stir-Fry

This dish is a lovely mix of fresh vegetables packed full of flavor. This recipe makes a large quantity, but it can easily be cut in half if need be, or you could set the leftovers aside for an upcoming meal.

PREP TIME: 10 minutes   **COOK TIME: 18 minutes**   **SERVES: 6**

2 tablespoons olive oil, divided

1 pound red potatoes, diced

1 pound baby portobello mushrooms, sliced

1 pound asparagus, trimmed and cut into 2-inch pieces

1 medium red onion, peeled and sliced

1 medium red bell pepper, seeded and sliced

3/4 teaspoon kosher salt

1/2 teaspoon ground black pepper

6 cloves garlic, peeled and minced

3 tablespoons balsamic vinegar

2 tablespoons Italian seasoning

1. Preheat griddle to medium. Add 1 tablespoon oil, a squirt of water, and potatoes. Cover with a melting dome or lid and cook 7 minutes. Remove dome a few times during the cooking time to flip potatoes and add more water before covering again.

2. Remove dome and set aside. Add remaining 1 tablespoon oil, mushrooms, asparagus, onion, bell pepper, salt, and black pepper. Cook 7 more minutes, stirring a few times with spatulas.

3. Add garlic, vinegar, and Italian seasoning. Cook 4 more minutes, tossing. Serve warm.

PER SERVING

Calories: **147**

Fat: **3g**

Protein: **5g**

Sodium: **258mg**

Fiber: **4g**

Carbohydrates: **25g**

Sugar: **6g**

Asparagus Tomato Panzanella

This colorful salad has a bright homemade dressing. It's a nice, light summer dinner option, or you could bring it to a party as a side dish. Feel free to add more garlic toast if you like.

PREP TIME: 10 minutes   **COOK TIME: 13 minutes**   **SERVES: 4**

1/2 cup olive oil

1/4 cup balsamic vinegar

1 tablespoon Dijon mustard

1 teaspoon Italian seasoning

4 slices frozen garlic toast, thawed

1 pound asparagus, trimmed end cut into 2-inch pieces

1 pint grape tomatoes (whole)

8 ounces baby portobello mushrooms, sliced

1/2 teaspoon kosher salt

1/4 teaspoon ground black pepper

4 ounces crumbled goat cheese

Trimming Asparagus

The bottom few inches of asparagus are often tough. To trim the tough part away, hold one piece of asparagus and slightly bend it. The asparagus will naturally snap, separating where it becomes tough. Hold that piece of asparagus next to the rest of the bunch to determine where to trim the remaining pieces.

1. To make dressing, in a small bowl, whisk oil, vinegar, mustard, and Italian seasoning until combined. Set aside.
2. Preheat griddle to medium. Place garlic toast on griddle and cook 4 minutes, flipping a few times. Remove and, once cool, cut into cubes. Set aside.
3. Add 2 tablespoons of prepared dressing to griddle, along with asparagus, tomatoes, mushrooms, salt, and pepper. Cook 8–9 minutes, stirring with spatulas a few times, until vegetables are tender. Let cool slightly.
4. In a large bowl, place cubed bread, vegetables, and remaining dressing and toss until combined. Top with cheese before serving.

PER SERVING

Calories: **544**

Fat: **42g**

Protein: **13g**

Sodium: **726mg**

Fiber: **3g**

Carbohydrates: **28g**

Sugar: **7g**

Bang-Bang Ramen Noodles

This recipe makes a unique stir-fried noodle dish. If you want some crispy noodle bits, press the noodles down with spatulas on the flat top. Feel free to add tofu or some vegetables of your choice for a healthier, heartier dinner.

PREP TIME: **15 minutes**   COOK TIME: **10 minutes**   SERVES: **4**

4 (3-ounce) packages ramen noodles, noodles only (no flavor packet)

3/4 cup mayonnaise

3/4 cup Thai sweet chili sauce

3 tablespoons sriracha

1 tablespoon vegetable oil

1 medium yellow onion, peeled and diced

6 cloves garlic, peeled and minced

1/2 teaspoon kosher salt

6 medium scallions, sliced

2 tablespoons lemon juice

1. Bring a large pot of water to a boil over high heat. Add noodles and boil for 2 minutes. Drain and rinse well with cold water.
2. To make bang-bang sauce, in a medium bowl, stir mayonnaise, sweet chili sauce, and sriracha until combined.
3. Preheat griddle to medium. Add oil and onion and cook 3 minutes. Add noodles, half of prepared bang-bang sauce, garlic, and salt. Cook 5 minutes, tossing with spatulas.
4. Add scallions, lemon juice, and remaining sauce. Mix until combined, 1–2 more minutes, before serving.

PER SERVING
Calories: **650**
Fat: **40g**
Protein: **6g**

Sodium: **1,717mg**
Fiber: **2g**
Carbohydrates: **63g**
Sugar: **31g**

Eggplant Parmesan

This classic dish can be made quickly on the flat top. Try serving this over pasta or zucchini noodles for a complete meal.

PREP TIME: 35 minutes*   **COOK TIME: 10 minutes**   **SERVES: 4**

1 teaspoon kosher salt, divided

2 small eggplants, cut horizontally into 8 total ($\frac{1}{2}$-inch) slices

$\frac{1}{4}$ cup all-purpose flour

1 large egg, beaten

$\frac{1}{2}$ cup Italian bread crumbs

$\frac{1}{4}$ cup grated vegetarian Parmesan cheese

2 tablespoons olive oil

2 cups marinara sauce

2 cups shredded mozzarella cheese

8 basil leaves, sliced

The Perfect Eggplant

Picking a small to medium-sized eggplant that is still firm, not soft, works best for this dish. A green stem is often an indicator of the perfect eggplant. Salting the eggplant slices and drying them well draws out excess water, which results in a crisper, firmer texture.

1. Sprinkle $\frac{1}{2}$ teaspoon salt on eggplant slices and place on a tray. Let this sit on the countertop for 20 minutes.
2. Set out three shallow dishes. Place flour in one, egg in another, and in the third combine bread crumbs, Parmesan, and remaining $\frac{1}{2}$ teaspoon salt.
3. Pat eggplant very dry. Dip each slice into flour to lightly coat, then into egg, and lastly into bread crumb mixture, coating both sides well.
4. Preheat griddle to medium. Add oil and place eggplant slices on the Blackstone for 4 minutes per side.
5. Spoon some marinara sauce over each slice and sprinkle mozzarella over top. Cover with melting dome or lid and cook for 2 minutes.
6. Remove dome and set aside. Garnish with basil and serve right away.

*Includes resting time.

PER SERVING

Calories: **453**
Fat: **21g**
Protein: **21g**
Sodium: **1,529mg**
Fiber: **10g**
Carbohydrates: **43g**
Sugar: **16g**

Eggplant Quinoa Bowls

Enjoy this fresh vegetable stir-fry served on top of cooked quinoa for a complete, healthy meal. Add mushrooms, zucchini, or any other vegetables you like, and experiment with serving the vegetables over cooked couscous or rice instead of quinoa.

PREP TIME: 15 minutes   **COOK TIME: 10 minutes**   **SERVES: 4**

$1^{1}/3$ cups quinoa

2 tablespoons olive oil

1 medium red onion, peeled and sliced

1 medium eggplant, cut into 1-inch pieces

8 ounces spinach, chopped

4 cloves garlic, peeled and minced

$1/2$ tablespoon Italian seasoning

$1/2$ teaspoon kosher salt

$1/4$ teaspoon ground black pepper

$1/2$ cup sliced sun-dried tomatoes

$1/2$ cup shredded vegetarian Parmesan cheese

$1/4$ cup toasted pine nuts

1 tablespoon lemon juice

1. In a saucepan, combine quinoa with $2^{2}/3$ cups water. Bring to a boil, then simmer, uncovered, until liquid is absorbed, about 12 minutes. Cover and set aside.

2. Preheat griddle to medium. Add oil, onion, and eggplant. Cook 5 minutes, mixing with spatulas a few times.

3. Add spinach, garlic, Italian seasoning, salt, and pepper. Mix together and cook 4 minutes.

4. Add sun-dried tomatoes, cheese, pine nuts, and lemon juice. Cook 1 more minute.

5. Serve in bowls over cooked quinoa.

PER SERVING

Calories: **423**

Fat: **14g**

Protein: **18g**

Sodium: **487mg**

Fiber: **12g**

Carbohydrates: **59g**

Sugar: **11g**

Cauliflower Steaks with Cowboy Butter

I don't know where cowboy butter got its name, but it makes me want to say "Yee-haw!" It's a buttery blend with spices, herbs, and lemon to cut through the richness. Make a double batch and store it in the refrigerator to use when the mood strikes.

PREP TIME: 10 minutes   **COOK TIME: 10 minutes**   **SERVES: 4**

1 stick unsalted butter, softened

1 tablespoon lemon juice

1 tablespoon Dijon mustard

$1/2$ teaspoon paprika

$1/2$ teaspoon garlic powder

$1/2$ teaspoon dried parsley

$1/2$ teaspoon dried thyme

1 large head cauliflower, stems and leaves removed, sliced vertically into 4 ($1^1/2$-inch-thick) steaks

1 tablespoon olive oil

$1/2$ teaspoon kosher salt

$1/4$ teaspoon ground black pepper

1. To make cowboy butter, put butter, lemon juice, mustard, paprika, garlic powder, parsley, and thyme in a small bowl. Stir until combined. Set aside.

2. Brush cauliflower slices with oil and season with salt and pepper on both sides.

3. Preheat griddle to medium. Place cauliflower on the Blackstone and cook 5 minutes per side. Serve with dollops of prepared cowboy butter on top.

Cauliflower Steak Tips

Try buying two heads of cauliflower and cutting two cauliflower steaks from the center of each. Then put them in a food processor and pulse for a few seconds. You now have cauliflower rice that you can store in a sealable plastic bag in the refrigerator for a few days, or in the freezer for a few months.

PER SERVING

Calories: **288**

Fat: **25g**

Protein: **5g**

Sodium: **399mg**

Fiber: **4g**

Carbohydrates: **12g**

Sugar: **4g**

Goat Cheese Vegetable Sliders

These colorful sliders are a nice dinner, but they could also be served as a meatless appetizer or game-day snack. Don't like goat cheese? Replace it with feta or a few extra slices of provolone.

PREP TIME: **15 minutes**　　COOK TIME: **10 minutes**　　SERVES: **4**

2 tablespoons olive oil

1 medium red bell pepper, seeded and diced

1 medium yellow bell pepper, seeded and diced

1 small red onion, peeled and diced

1 small eggplant, diced

1 pint cherry tomatoes (whole)

$1/2$ teaspoon kosher salt

$1/4$ teaspoon ground black pepper

6 cloves garlic, peeled and minced

2 tablespoons balsamic vinegar

1 tablespoon Italian seasoning

1 (12-count) package slider buns, not separated, sliced horizontally to separate tops from bottoms

1 ounce balsamic glaze

6 (1-ounce) slices provolone cheese

4 ounces crumbled goat cheese

6 basil leaves, sliced

1. Preheat griddle to medium. Add oil, bell peppers, onion, eggplant, tomatoes, salt, and black pepper. Cook 5 minutes, mixing with spatulas a few times.

2. Add garlic, vinegar, and Italian seasoning. Cook 4 more minutes, stirring.

3. Move vegetables to one side of griddle, scrape center clean, and turn heat off. Place both bun halves, cut sides down, on the griddle for a few seconds until toasted to your desired darkness. Flip bottom bun half and add vegetables, balsamic glaze, provolone, goat cheese, and basil. Add the top bun half and press down slightly. Cover with melting dome or lid for 1 more minute until cheese is melted. Cut into individual buns before serving.

PER SERVING

Calories: **710**

Fat: **30g**

Protein: **32g**

Sodium: **1,160mg**

Fiber: **9g**

Carbohydrates: **82g**

Sugar: **26g**

Spinach Mushroom Feta Ravioli

This is a tasty pasta dish with a Greek twist! It is full of flavor and easy to make, and the leftovers are even better reheated the next day. Don't like feta? Top with vegetarian Parmesan cheese instead.

PREP TIME: 10 minutes   **COOK TIME: 13 minutes**   **SERVES: 4**

1 (20-ounce) bag frozen cheese ravioli, thawed

1 tablespoon olive oil

1 medium yellow onion, peeled and diced

8 ounces baby portobello mushrooms, sliced

1 teaspoon dried oregano

1/2 teaspoon kosher salt

1/4 teaspoon ground black pepper

8 ounces spinach, chopped

6 cloves garlic, peeled and minced

1 (24-ounce) jar marinara sauce

6 ounces crumbled feta cheese

1. Preheat griddle to medium. Add ravioli, squirt 2 tablespoons water over top, and cover with a melting dome or lid. Cook 3 minutes, tossing halfway through the cooking time and adding 2 more tablespoons water before covering again.

2. Remove dome and set aside. Add oil, onion, mushrooms, oregano, salt, and pepper. Cook 5 minutes, stirring with spatulas.

3. Add spinach and garlic and cook 3 more minutes.

4. Pour marinara sauce over top and cook 1–2 more minutes, mixing together. Serve topped with cheese.

PER SERVING

Calories: **542**

Fat: **24g**

Protein: **23g**

Sodium: **1,536mg**

Fiber: **5g**

Carbohydrates: **58g**

Sugar: **11g**

CHAPTER 9

Desserts

When most people think of griddle cooking, they might not think of desserts, but the truth is you can cook so many sweet treats on your Blackstone! The griddle is an ideal place for cooking cakes, brownies, and even roasted fruits. In this chapter you will find all the sweet treats that will cure your sugar cravings. With recipes ranging from Peanut Butter Brownies and Bananas Foster to Cookies 'n' Cream Cakes, S'mores Donut Melts, and Strawberry Chocolate Hazelnut Crepes, the mouthwatering delights in this chapter are guaranteed to hit the sweet spot—no matter what you are craving!

Peanut Butter Brownies

Warm, ooey gooey brownies with melty peanut butter cup centers! This rich dessert on the Blackstone is sure to be a family favorite. You will need ten (4-inch) silicone egg rings and nonstick cooking spray, plus eggs and vegetable oil to prepare the brownie batter.

PREP TIME: 10 minutes   **COOK TIME: 14 minutes**   **SERVES: 10**

1 (20-ounce) box brownie mix, batter prepared according to package directions

10 regular-sized chocolate peanut butter cups

PER SERVING

Calories: 458
Fat: 21g
Protein: 5g
Sodium: 278mg
Fiber: 2g
Carbohydrates: 60g
Sugar: 44g

1. Preheat griddle to lowest heat setting. Place ten egg rings on the Blackstone and spray well with nonstick cooking spray. Divide brownie batter evenly into each ring and top with a peanut butter cup.
2. Cover with a melting dome or lid. Cook 12–14 minutes until brownies are set.
3. Remove dome and set aside. Gently lift egg rings up and use spatula to transfer brownies to a tray. Serve.

S'mores Cones

Kids will love to help make this dessert. It's a fun twist on traditional s'mores, using ice cream cones in place of graham crackers. Use waffle cones for a jumbo version.

PREP TIME: 10 minutes   **COOK TIME: 5 minutes**   **SERVES: 8**

8 sugar cones

1 cup mini marshmallows

1 cup chocolate chips

PER SERVING

Calories: 172
Fat: 6g
Protein: 3g
Sodium: 51mg
Fiber: 1g
Carbohydrates: 26g
Sugar: 17g

1. Evenly distribute marshmallows and chocolate chips among the cones, alternating marshmallows and chocolate chips and smashing them down gently to fit as much as possible in each. Wrap each cone individually in foil.
2. Preheat griddle to medium-low. Place foil packets on the Blackstone for 5 minutes, turning with tongs a few times. Unwrap and let cool slightly before serving.

Bourbon Peaches and Pound Cake

The bourbon in this recipe adds flavor, but you can certainly leave it out if you prefer. Peaches that are ripe but still firm work best for this dish. This is delicious topped with plenty of whipped cream.

PREP TIME: 5 minutes   **COOK TIME: 8 minutes**   **SERVES: 4**

4 medium peaches, pitted and sliced

4 tablespoons unsalted butter, divided

2 tablespoons bourbon

3 tablespoons light brown sugar

$1/4$ teaspoon ground cinnamon

4 (1-inch-thick) slices pound cake

1. Preheat griddle to medium-low. Add peach slices and 3 tablespoons butter. Cook 3 minutes, mixing a few times with spatulas.
2. Add bourbon, brown sugar, and cinnamon to peaches. Cook 2–3 more minutes until peaches are tender and sauce is caramelized.
3. As the peaches cook, add remaining 1 tablespoon butter to an empty space on the Blackstone. Once melted, place pound cake on it. Cook 1 minute per side and remove once toasted how you like.
4. Serve bourbon peaches on top of pound cake.

PER SERVING

Calories: **377**

Fat: **15g**

Protein: **4g**

Sodium: **188mg**

Fiber: **3g**

Carbohydrates: **53g**

Sugar: **41g**

Strawberry Chocolate Hazelnut Crepes

With this basic batter, you can make dessert crepes to fill or top with anything you like. Add a dollop of whipped cream and a mint leaf for an elegant presentation.

PREP TIME: 15 minutes*   **COOK TIME: 8 minutes**   **SERVES: 8**

3 large eggs, at room temperature

1$\frac{1}{2}$ cups whole milk, at room temperature

1 cup all-purpose flour

2 tablespoons granulated sugar

4 tablespoons unsalted butter, melted, divided

1 teaspoon vanilla extract

$\frac{1}{4}$ teaspoon kosher salt

1 cup chocolate hazelnut spread, warmed slightly

$\frac{1}{2}$ tablespoon confectioners' sugar

1 pint strawberries, stems removed, sliced

Storing Leftover Crepes

Cooked crepes store better than batter does, so make the entire batch of crepes, even if you won't be filling them all in one day. Store any extras in a sealable plastic bag with parchment paper in between to separate them. Refrigerate for up to 3 days or freeze for up to 3 months. Reheat before filling and serving.

1. Crack eggs into a medium bowl and beat with a fork. Add milk, flour, granulated sugar, 2 tablespoons butter, vanilla, and salt. Whisk until combined and then let rest 10 minutes.
2. Preheat griddle to medium. Brush some of remaining melted butter on griddle. Start a batch of 4 crepes by pouring 4 ($\frac{1}{4}$-cup) puddles of batter on griddle, leaving room between crepes to spread batter out. Use spatulas to keep the batter in circles if needed and spread it as thin as possible. Cook 1–2 minutes per side until golden brown.
3. Remove crepes and repeat process to make 4 more crepes.
4. Drizzle warm chocolate hazelnut spread on crepes, fold each into fourths, and top with confectioners' sugar and sliced strawberries before serving.

*Includes resting time.

PER SERVING

Calories: 382

Fat: 19g

Protein: 9g

Sodium: 122mg

Fiber: 2g

Carbohydrates: 43g

Sugar: 29g

Caramel Apple Wonton Nachos

This dessert is messy, but that's just part of the fun. Top the wonton "chips" right before serving so they stay crisp. Add a sprinkle of sea salt for some salted caramel vibes, and whipped cream is also a plus.

PREP TIME: **10 minutes**   COOK TIME: **11 minutes**   SERVES: **4**

2 tablespoons vegetable oil

12 wonton wrappers, cut in half diagonally

$1/2$ tablespoon granulated sugar

2 medium Honeycrisp apples (with peel), cored and diced

4 tablespoons unsalted butter

3 tablespoons light brown sugar

$1/4$ teaspoon ground cinnamon

2 ounces caramel sauce

Making Crispy Wonton Wrappers

Cook a test wonton chip before putting all of them on the griddle. That way you will have a better idea exactly how they cook. Also, use the tongs to press the wontons against the flat top. This will help them cook more evenly.

1. Preheat griddle to medium. Add oil and wonton wrappers. Cook 2–3 minutes total, flipping with tongs a few times. Remove once crisped to your liking and sprinkle with granulated sugar right away. Set aside.

2. Put apples on Blackstone. Cook 4 minutes, tossing a few times with spatulas. Add butter, brown sugar, and cinnamon. Cook 4 more minutes, stirring.

3. Top wonton chips with apple mixture, drizzle with caramel sauce, and serve right away.

PER SERVING
Calories: **347**
Fat: **16g**
Protein: **3g**

Sodium: **191mg**
Fiber: **3g**
Carbohydrates: **47g**
Sugar: **21g**

Lemon Blueberry Cakes

Mini cakes cooked on the Blackstone make adorable individual desserts. You will need sixteen silicone egg rings for these. Depending on how many you have, you may need to cook these cakes in a few batches. Eggs and vegetable oil will also be needed for the cake batter.

PREP TIME: 10 minutes   **COOK TIME: 13 minutes**   **SERVES: 16**

1 (13.25-ounce) box lemon cake mix, batter prepared according to package directions

1 pint blueberries

1 (16-ounce) container vanilla frosting

1. Preheat griddle to lowest heat setting. Place sixteen silicone egg rings on the Blackstone and spray well with nonstick spray. Fill each ring half full of cake batter and add a few blueberries.
2. Cover with a melting dome or lid for 11–13 minutes until cake is set. Remove dome and set aside. Gently pull egg rings up to remove them. Use a spatula to transfer cakes to a tray.
3. Let cakes cool completely and then spread frosting on each before serving.

PER SERVING   Sodium: **240mg**
Calories: **270**   Fiber: **0g**
Fat: **11g**   Carbohydrates: **42g**
Protein: **2g**   Sugar: **30g**

Cherry Cheesecake Quesadillas

Here is all the yumminess of cherry cheesecake sandwiched inside of a crispy, golden tortilla cooked to perfection on the Blackstone griddle.

PREP TIME: 5 minutes   **COOK TIME: 6 minutes**   **SERVES: 6**

3 (10-inch) flour tortillas

2 cups cheesecake filling

1 tablespoon unsalted butter

1 (20-ounce) can cherry pie filling

1 tablespoon confectioners' sugar

Cheesecake Filling Options

You have two options for easy cheesecake filling. Most large grocery stores now sell tubs of pre-made, already-cooked cheesecake filling. Another option is to buy a box of no-bake cheesecake mix. For this, simply follow the package directions, which typically require a hand mixer and some milk.

1. Lay tortillas flat on a work surface and spread cheesecake filling evenly on one half of each tortilla.

2. Preheat griddle to medium-low. Add butter and, once melted, put tortillas on Blackstone, cheesecake sides up. Spoon some cherry pie filling on top of each tortilla's filling. Use a spatula to fold each tortilla's empty half over the filled half, forming a half-moon shape.

3. Cook 2–3 minutes per side until tortillas are crisped to perfection.

4. Cut each half-moon in half and sprinkle with confectioners' sugar before serving.

PER SERVING

Calories: **555**

Fat: **27g**

Protein: **9g**

Sodium: **672mg**

Fiber: **1g**

Carbohydrates: **70g**

Sugar: **23g**

Bananas Foster

Use your spatulas to keep the sauce together on the Blackstone. For extra flair, you can use a grill lighter to ignite the rum after adding it. Serve over vanilla ice cream, pound cake, or French toast.

PREP TIME: 5 minutes   **COOK TIME: 5 minutes**   **SERVES: 4**

5 tablespoons unsalted butter

1/3 cup light brown sugar

2 medium ripe bananas, peeled and sliced

1/2 teaspoon ground cinnamon

2 ounces dark rum

1. Preheat griddle to medium. Add butter and, just as it starts to melt, brown sugar. Cook 1 minute, mixing together.
2. Add bananas and cook 2 more minutes, mixing with spatulas.
3. Add cinnamon and rum and cook 1–2 more minutes until mixture is saucy and caramelized. Serve.

PER SERVING
Calories: **253**
Fat: **12g**
Protein: **1g**
Sodium: **7mg**
Fiber: **2g**
Carbohydrates: **32g**
Sugar: **25g**

Lemon Strawberry Shortcake

The lemon in this dessert really brightens up the flavors. For even more lemony goodness, you can use lemon pound cake.

PREP TIME: 5 minutes   **COOK TIME: 5 minutes**   **SERVES: 4**

1 pint strawberries, stems removed, sliced

1 tablespoon granulated sugar

1 tablespoon lemon juice

1/2 teaspoon lemon zest

4 (1-inch-thick) slices pound cake

2 ounces whipped cream

1. Preheat griddle to medium-low. Add strawberries and cook 1 minute, tossing with spatulas.
2. Add sugar, lemon juice, and lemon zest. Cook 4 more minutes, stirring. During the last 2 minutes of cooking time, put pound cake on an empty space on the Blackstone and cook 1 minute per side.
3. Serve strawberries over cake, topped with whipped cream.

PER SERVING
Calories: **244**
Fat: **9g**
Protein: **3g**
Sodium: **186mg**
Fiber: **2g**
Carbohydrates: **37g**
Sugar: **24g**

Pineapple Sunshine Cakes

These beautiful and tasty mini cakes are sure to boost your mood with a ray of sunshine. You may need to make them in batches, depending on how many silicone egg rings you have.

PREP TIME: 10 minutes   **COOK TIME: 13 minutes**   **SERVES: 16**

2 (8-ounce) cans crushed pineapple, divided

1 (13.25-ounce) box yellow cake mix, batter prepared according to package directions

1 (8-ounce) container frozen whipped topping, thawed

1 (3.4-ounce) box instant vanilla pudding mix

16 maraschino cherries

Elevating Boxed Cake Mix

You can certainly use a homemade cake batter in place of the mix, but if you opt for a boxed mix, here are some tricks to make it taste homemade: Add an extra egg, use whole milk in place of water, and use softened butter in place of vegetable oil—easy substitutions to create an even tastier cake!

1. Fold one can of pineapple into prepared cake batter.
2. Preheat griddle to lowest heat setting. Place sixteen silicone egg rings on griddle and spray well with nonstick cooking spray. Fill each egg ring $2/3$ full of batter, cover with melting dome or lid, and cook 11–13 minutes until cake is set.
3. Remove dome and set aside. Gently lift egg rings up and use spatula to transfer cakes to a tray. Let cool completely.
4. In a medium bowl, mix together whipped topping, pudding mix, and remaining can of pineapple. Spread mixture over cooled cakes and top each with a cherry.

PER SERVING

Calories: 241
Fat: **10g**
Protein: **2g**
Sodium: **206mg**
Fiber: **1g**
Carbohydrates: **35g**
Sugar: **13g**

Churro Bites

This delicious, cinnamon and sugar–coated dessert can now be cooked on your griddle. With a simple tube of biscuit dough you can make these treats quickly and easily any time you want!

PREP TIME: 10 minutes   **COOK TIME: 8 minutes**   **SERVES: 4**

1 (7.5-ounce, 10 count) tube refrigerated biscuits

1/4 cup granulated sugar

2 teaspoons ground cinnamon

3 tablespoons unsalted butter, divided

1/4 cup chocolate sauce

1. Cut each biscuit into fourths. To a medium bowl, add sugar and cinnamon and stir until combined.
2. Preheat griddle to medium-low. Add 1 tablespoon butter and, once melted, place biscuit pieces on Blackstone. Cook 7–8 minutes, flipping a few times with tongs until golden brown. Add remaining 2 tablespoons butter and toss with spatulas just until biscuits are coated.
3. Transfer biscuits to bowl with cinnamon-sugar mixture and toss until coated. Serve with chocolate sauce for dipping.

PER SERVING   Sodium: **520mg**
Calories: **312**   Fiber: **2g**
Fat: **9g**   Carbohydrates: **51g**
Protein: **4g**   Sugar: **22g**

Cinnamon Apple Tacos

Who would have thought of tacos for dessert?! Such a fun and kind of messy experience, but in the best way possible. Placing parchment paper between the rolls and your burger press helps prevent sticking.

PREP TIME: 10 minutes   **COOK TIME: 12 minutes**   **SERVES: 5**

2 medium Honeycrisp apples (with peel), cored and diced

4 tablespoons unsalted butter

3 tablespoons light brown sugar

1/2 teaspoon ground cinnamon

1 (17.5-ounce) tube refrigerated jumbo cinnamon rolls (5-count), with icing

1. Preheat griddle to medium. Put apples on Blackstone and cook 4 minutes, tossing a few times with spatulas. Add butter, brown sugar, and cinnamon. Cook 4 more minutes, mixing with spatulas. Remove and set aside. Scrape griddle and lower heat to medium-low.

2. Place cinnamon rolls on Blackstone, spaced 3 inches apart. Use a burger press to smash them flat. Cook 2 minutes, flip, and smash them again. Cook 2 more minutes or until dough is cooked through. During the last minute of cooking time, place the cup of icing that came with cinnamon rolls on the griddle to warm (place it on the edge of the griddle where the heat is lower so the plastic does not melt).

3. Evenly distribute apples on top of cinnamon rolls, drizzle with icing, and serve folded up like a taco.

PER SERVING

Calories: **469**

Fat: **11g**

Protein: **5g**

Sodium: **777mg**

Fiber: **3g**

Carbohydrates: **71g**

Sugar: **36g**

S'mores Donut Melts

These dessert sandwiches are messy and fun to eat: a slight crunch from the graham cracker, plus gooey marshmallow chocolatey goodness. You can also place the donut halves on the griddle cut-side down if you like to keep your hands a bit less sticky as you eat. As a variation of this recipe, try replacing the chocolate with a chocolate peanut butter cup.

PREP TIME: 5 minutes   **COOK TIME: 5 minutes**   **SERVES: 4**

2 tablespoons unsalted butter

4 glazed donuts, cut in half to separate tops and bottoms

4 rectangular graham crackers

4 (4-inch) chocolate bars

32 mini marshmallows

1. Preheat griddle to medium-low. Add butter and, once melted, place the 4 bottom donut halves on griddle, cut sides up.

2. On each, place a graham cracker, a chocolate bar, and 8 mini marshmallows. Top with the top half of each donut, cut-side down. Press down slightly. Cover with melting dome or lid for 2 minutes.

3. Remove dome and set aside. Flip and cook 2–3 more minutes until donut is golden brown and filling is melted. Serve warm.

PER SERVING

Calories: **295**

Fat: **22g**

Protein: **5g**

Sodium: **236mg**

Fiber: **1g**

Carbohydrates: **49g**

Sugar: **28g**

Cherry Brownies

Top these brownies with ice cream for an even more decadent experience. You will need ten (4-inch) silicone egg rings and nonstick cooking spray, plus eggs and vegetable oil to prepare the brownie batter.

PREP TIME: **10 minutes**   COOK TIME: **12 minutes**   SERVES: **10**

1 (20-ounce) box brownie mix, batter prepared according to package directions

30 maraschino cherries, cut in half

PER SERVING
Calories: **377**
Fat: **15g**
Protein: **3g**
Sodium: **211mg**
Fiber: **1g**
Carbohydrates: **54g**
Sugar: **39g**

1. Preheat griddle to lowest heat setting. Place ten egg rings on the Blackstone and spray well with nonstick cooking spray. Pour in brownie batter, filling each ring ³⁄4 full, and add 6 cherry halves to each.
2. Cover with a melting dome or lid and cook 12–14 minutes until brownies are set.
3. Remove dome and set aside. Gently lift egg rings up and use spatula to transfer brownies to a tray. Serve.

Brown Sugar Cinnamon Pineapple

This sweet fruit treat gets nice and caramelized on the griddle thanks to the brown sugar. You could also serve this over a scoop of vanilla ice cream.

PREP TIME: **10 minutes**   COOK TIME: **5 minutes**   SERVES: **4**

1 ripe pineapple, peeled, cored, and sliced lengthwise into 8 (2-inch-thick) strips

3 tablespoons light brown sugar

1 teaspoon ground cinnamon

2 tablespoons unsalted butter

PER SERVING
Calories: **191**
Fat: **4g**
Protein: **1g**
Sodium: **5mg**
Fiber: **4g**
Carbohydrates: **40g**
Sugar: **32g**

1. Place pineapple strips on a tray and sprinkle all sides with brown sugar and cinnamon.
2. Preheat griddle to medium-low. Put butter on the Blackstone and, once melted, add pineapple strips. Cook 5 minutes total, flipping a few times. Serve warm.

Salted Caramel Bread Pudding

This recipe features bread pudding cooked on the griddle with a delicious homemade salted caramel sauce drizzled on top. This is also amazing topped with more kosher salt and whipped cream.

PREP TIME: 15 minutes*   **COOK TIME: 8 minutes**   **SERVES: 10**

2 sticks plus 2 tablespoons unsalted butter, divided

1 cup light brown sugar

1 teaspoon kosher salt

1 quart half-and-half

4 large eggs

$1/2$ cup granulated sugar

1 teaspoon vanilla extract

1 (16-ounce) loaf brioche, cubed

Bread Pudding Variations

Adding $1/2$ cup of raisins and 2 tablespoons of rum to this batter is an incredible recipe twist. For another variation, just add 2 tablespoons of bourbon. For a simplified version, feel free to use a store-bought caramel sauce sprinkled with flaky sea salt.

1. To a medium saucepan add 2 sticks butter, brown sugar, and salt. Place on the stove over medium heat. Once butter is melted, cook 5 minutes, whisking a few times. Remove and set aside.
2. To a large bowl add half-and-half, eggs, granulated sugar, and vanilla. Whisk until combined. Fold in bread cubes and let sit 5 minutes.
3. Preheat griddle to medium-low. Add remaining 2 tablespoons butter to griddle and, once melted, scoop 10 piles of bread pudding batter onto the Blackstone, leaving about 3 inches between each scoop. Cook 3–4 minutes per side or until golden brown.
4. Serve warm, drizzled with prepared caramel sauce.

*Includes resting time.

PER SERVING
Calories: **573**
Fat: **31g**
Protein: **9g**
Sodium: **495mg**
Fiber: **0g**
Carbohydrates: **61g**
Sugar: **39g**

Cookies 'n' Cream Cakes

This is a chocolate lover's dream come true. Individual cakes on the Blackstone are great for serving a crowd. You may need to make these in a few batches.

PREP TIME: 10 minutes   **COOK TIME: 13 minutes**   **SERVES: 16**

1 (13.25-ounce) box devil's food cake mix, batter prepared according to package directions

20 chocolate sandwich cookies, divided

1 (16-ounce) container vanilla frosting

Making Them Festive

You can mix up the cake and frosting flavors on these cakes for different holidays and seasons. For Halloween, use chocolate frosting and spooky-themed sprinkles. Spring cakes are great with vanilla cake and frosting, vanilla sandwich cookies, and pastel sprinkles. For the winter holidays use red and green sprinkles or white and blue confetti candy to bring snowy vibes.

1. Preheat griddle to lowest heat setting. Place sixteen silicone egg rings on griddle and spray well with nonstick cooking spray. Fill each egg ring half full of batter and place a chocolate sandwich cookie in center of each. Cover with melting dome or lid and cook 11–13 minutes until cake is set.
2. Remove dome and set aside. Gently lift egg rings up and use spatula to transfer cakes to a tray. Let cool completely.
3. Spread frosting on top of cakes. Crush remaining 4 cookies and sprinkle crumbs over frosting before serving.

PER SERVING
Calories: **347**
Fat: **16g**
Protein: **3g**

Sodium: **324mg**
Fiber: **1g**
Carbohydrates: **49g**
Sugar: **34g**

"Elvis" Donut Sandwiches

It's well known that Elvis's favorite sandwich was peanut butter and banana. This sweet version on the flat top gets melty and decadent.

PREP TIME: **5 minutes**   COOK TIME: **6 minutes**   SERVES: **4**

4 glazed donuts, cut in half to separate tops and bottoms

1/2 cup peanut butter

1 medium ripe banana, peeled and sliced

2 tablespoons unsalted butter

1. Lay all donut halves cut-side down on a work surface and spread peanut butter on each. Add sliced bananas to 4 of the donut halves. Top with 4 remaining donut halves, cut-side up.
2. Preheat griddle to medium-low. Add butter and, once melted, place sandwiches on the Blackstone. Cook 2–3 minutes per side until donuts are crisped and golden brown. Serve warm.

PER SERVING

Calories: **444**

Fat: **31g**

Protein: **10g**

Sodium: **150mg**

Fiber: **3g**

Carbohydrates: **31g**

Sugar: **14g**

Honey Cinnamon Peaches with Mascarpone

This company-worthy elegant dessert is simple to prepare. Garnish with fresh mint leaves for extra zip. If you don't like mascarpone, use whipped cream instead.

PREP TIME: **5 minutes**   COOK TIME: **6 minutes**   SERVES: **6**

2 tablespoons unsalted butter

3 medium ripe peaches, cut in half, pits removed

1 teaspoon ground cinnamon

3 tablespoons honey, divided

6 ounces mascarpone

1. Preheat griddle to medium. Add butter and, once melted, place peach halves cut-side down on griddle. Cook 4 minutes.
2. Flip peaches, sprinkle with cinnamon, and drizzle with 1 1/2 tablespoons honey. Flip them back over and cook 1–2 minutes to allow the honey to caramelize.
3. Serve peaches topped with mascarpone and drizzled with remaining 1 1/2 tablespoons honey.

PER SERVING

Calories: **174**

Fat: **11g**

Protein: **3g**

Sodium: **16mg**

Fiber: **1g**

Carbohydrates: **19g**

Sugar: **16g**

STANDARD US/METRIC
MEASUREMENT CONVERSIONS

VOLUME CONVERSIONS

US Volume Measure	Metric Equivalent
⅛ teaspoon	0.5 milliliter
¼ teaspoon	1 milliliter
½ teaspoon	2 milliliters
1 teaspoon	5 milliliters
½ tablespoon	7 milliliters
1 tablespoon (3 teaspoons)	15 milliliters
2 tablespoons (1 fluid ounce)	30 milliliters
¼ cup (4 tablespoons)	60 milliliters
⅓ cup	90 milliliters
½ cup (4 fluid ounces)	125 milliliters
⅔ cup	160 milliliters
¾ cup (6 fluid ounces)	180 milliliters
1 cup (16 tablespoons)	250 milliliters
1 pint (2 cups)	500 milliliters
1 quart (4 cups)	1 liter (about)

WEIGHT CONVERSIONS

US Weight Measure	Metric Equivalent
½ ounce	15 grams
1 ounce	30 grams
2 ounces	60 grams
3 ounces	85 grams
¼ pound (4 ounces)	115 grams
½ pound (8 ounces)	225 grams
¾ pound (12 ounces)	340 grams
1 pound (16 ounces)	454 grams

OVEN TEMPERATURE CONVERSIONS

Degrees Fahrenheit	Degrees Celsius
200 degrees F	95 degrees C
250 degrees F	120 degrees C
275 degrees F	135 degrees C
300 degrees F	150 degrees C
325 degrees F	160 degrees C
350 degrees F	180 degrees C
375 degrees F	190 degrees C
400 degrees F	205 degrees C
425 degrees F	220 degrees C
450 degrees F	230 degrees C

BAKING PAN SIZES

American	Metric
8 × 1½ inch round baking pan	20 × 4 cm cake tin
9 × 1½ inch round baking pan	23 × 3.5 cm cake tin
11 × 7 × 1½ inch baking pan	28 × 18 × 4 cm baking tin
13 × 9 × 2 inch baking pan	30 × 20 × 5 cm baking tin
2 quart rectangular baking dish	30 × 20 × 3 cm baking tin
15 × 10 × 2 inch baking pan	30 × 25 × 2 cm baking tin (Swiss roll tin)
9 inch pie plate	22 × 4 or 23 × 4 cm pie plate
7 or 8 inch springform pan	18 or 20 cm springform or loose bottom cake tin
9 × 5 × 3 inch loaf pan	23 × 13 × 7 cm or 2 lb narrow loaf or pate tin
1½ quart casserole	1.5 liter casserole
2 quart casserole	2 liter casserole

Index